MW01596225

DARK PSYCHOLOGY AND MANIPULATION

Advanced techniques for controlling and reading people, learn the secrets and how to use mind control, empath, NLP, brainwashing, and covert persuasion.

Tony Clark

Table of Contents

INTRODUCTION..5

CHAPTER ONE...................................... 8

WHAT IS MANIPULATION?............................ 8

PSYCHOLOGICAL MANIPULATION 16

PSYCHOLOGICAL MANIPULATION
TECHNIQUES 17

CHAPTER TWO......................................21

CHARACTERISTICS OF EMOTIONAL &
PSYCHOLOGICAL ABUSE.................................21

USING MANIPULATIVE PSYCHOLOGY FOR
SELF-IMPROVEMENT 22

HOW PEOPLE ARE MANIPULATED
EMOTIONALLY AND WHY.............................. 26

DON'T BE PSYCHOLOGICALLY
MANIPULATED WHEN NEGOTIATING.........35

CHAPTER THREE............................. 40

HOW TO READ MINDS 40

MIND CONTROL AND ITS EFFECTS 43

LEARN THE ESSENCE OF MIND CONTROL 49

HOW TO MIND CONTROL - POWERFUL
TECHNIQUES FOR INFLUENCING PEOPLE 53

CHAPTER FOUR.. 63

EMOTIONAL-BEHAVIORAL PATTERNS....... 63

HOW TO READ PEOPLE 74

READ PEOPLE INSTANTLY - THE POWER OF
PERSUASION 78

MIND READING TECHNIQUE FOR YOU TO
TRY 80

CHAPTER FIVE.. 83

HOW TO CONTROL PEOPLE USING
HYPNOSIS 83

THE SECRET TRICKS TO READ PEOPLE'S
THOUGHTS 87

HOW TO IDENTIFY A MANIPULATOR 94

IS YOUR FRIEND MANIPULATING YOU? 98

CHAPTER SIX.. 109

MANIPULATION IN RELATIONSHIPS........ 109

ARE YOU A VICTIM OF AN EMOTIONAL
MANIPULATOR? 111

THE FOUR STYLES OF EMOTIONAL
MANIPULATION 115

PERSUASION AND MANIPULATION 120

CHAPTER SEVEN..125

HOW TO INFLUENCE PEOPLE SUCCESSFULLY 125

EMOTION OF OTHERS 129

HOW TO UNDERSTAND BODY LANGUAGE 134

LIST OF MANIPULATION TECHNIQUES ... 138

CHAPTER EIGHT 143

MANIPULATION TECHNIQUES 143

EMPATHIC ABILITIES 148

EMPATHIC PSYCHIC ABILITIES - PSYCHIC GUIDE 154

HOW TO MANIPULATE PEOPLE AND INFLUENCE DECISIONS 165

CHAPTER NINE 167

LEARN HOW TO MANIPULATE PEOPLE 167

THE DIFFERENCE BETWEEN MANIPULATING AND INSPIRING YOUR TARGET AUDIENCE1 169

HOW TO MANAGE MANIPULATIVE PEOPLE 173

CONCLUSION 181

INTRODUCTION

Copyright 2019 by **Tony Clark** – All rights reserved.

The brain is the headquarters post of each human activity; every single substantial activity discovers orders from the brain. The physical brain is separated into two hemispheres, in particular, the privilege and the left hemispheres; every hemisphere has one of a kind capacity for the complete body execution. The further hemisphere partition into littler organs, for example, the nerve center and the frontal cortex lobe, all who have unmistakable capacities for message relays and powerful brain neuron synthetic creation which are successful for better working of the brain. The mind then again is the impalpable part of the brain, the mind reasons, thinks, and acts in connection to the physical working of the brain. The mind states are characterized in two terms, which are the conscious mind and the intuitive mind. The conscious mind is the mindful part of the mind considerations prepared in this state of consciousness occurs in full familiarity with the individual concerned. Research has it that this part of the brain forms 10 percent of some random occasion. The intuitive mind then again spoke to the uninformed state of mind by definition, this part of the mind is covered from the conscious state. Incomprehensibly this state of mind forms more 90 percent of any occasion, this state of mind is increasingly alert when the conscious is very still. People who take part in how to peruse minds studies influence this part of the brain more.

Are mind-reading theories genuine?

An individual can peruse minds; anyway, the act in itself needs bunches of concentration and soul holding, for example, a person reading minds inevitably influences high frequency subliminally to connection holding with the contact person. The vast majority who can change this degree of concentration can convey productively through telepathy. Accomplishing this level needs direction and unbiased data and facts about how one can achieve the act. Preparing the mind to perform telepathy is conceivable through specific laws of attraction fits.

Laws of attraction and mind-reading

Law of attraction can be straightforward yet powerful in helping people achieve different self-development acts. Laws of attraction methods for performing self-development acts include individual actions, for example, positive reasoning. Your capacity in disclosing to yourself you can do inconceivabilities bends over to be the opening door for whatever activity you wish to influence. The vast majority known to do precise mind readings have different methods for deciphering a person's mind.

A portion of this people will center their mind to yours and through telepathy and other all-inclusive laws they can probably outline for in precision whatever you were supposing, others will pose inquiry arbitrarily and from that disclose to you things about your life. A few people will, in general, compare this to mystic's powers, they perhaps directly in some degree yet the sort of mind reading that originates from the law of an attraction is instinctive. Step by step instructions to peruse mind exercises can be achieved through concentration and figuring out how to tuning in to yourself first before you connect any outer mind readings.

CHAPTER ONE

What Is Manipulation?

Manipulation is the act of using aberrant tactics to control behavior, emotions, and relationships.

Most people take part in intermittent manipulation. For instance, telling an acquaintance, you feel "fine" when you are depressed is, in fact, a type of manipulation because it controls your acquaintance's perceptions of and reactions to you.

Manipulation can also have increasingly insidious consequences, be that as it may, and it is regularly associated with psychological mistreatment, especially in close relationships. Most people view manipulation adversely, especially when it harms the physical, enthusiastic, or emotional wellness of the person being manipulated.

While people who control others regularly do as such because they want to manage their condition and surroundings, an urge that frequently stems from profound seated dread or uneasiness, it's anything but a positive behavior. Taking part in manipulation may keep the controller from associating with their real self, and being manipulated can cause a person to encounter a wide scope of ill effects.

MANIPULATION AND MENTAL HEALTH

While most people take part in manipulation now and then, an endless example of manipulation can show a hidden psychological well-being concern.

Manipulation is especially regular with personality disorder diagnoses such as marginal personality (BPD) and narcissistic personality (NPD). For some with BPD, manipulation might be a means of gathering their passionate needs or acquiring approval, and it frequently occurs when the person with BPD feels insecure or deserted. As numerous people with BPD have witnessed or experienced abuse, manipulation may have created as a method for dealing with stress to get needs met in a roundabout way.

Individual with narcissistic personality (NPD) may have different reasons for taking part in manipulative behavior. As those with NPD may experience issues shaping close relationships, they may resort to manipulation to "keep" their partner in the relationship. Characteristics of narcissistic manipulation may incorporate shaming, accusing, playing the "person in question," control issues, and gaslighting.

Munchausen syndrome as a substitute, during which a parental figure makes another person sick to pick up consideration or warmth, is another condition that is described by manipulative behaviors.

MANIPULATION IN RELATIONSHIPS

Long haul manipulation can have severe effects in close relationships, including those between friends, relatives, and sentimental partners. Manipulation can crumble the health of a relationship and lead to the poor emotional wellness of those in the dissolution of the relationship or relationship

In partnership or In a marriage, manipulation can cause one partner to feel harassed, isolated, or worthless. Indeed, even in healthy relationships, one partner may incidentally control the other to stay away from showdown or also trying to shield their partner from inclination troubled. Numerous people may even realize they are being monitored in their relationship and choose to neglect or make light of it. Manipulation in personal relationships can take innumerable forms, including misrepresentation, blame, gift-giving or selectively showing friendship, secret-keeping, and passive aggression.

Parents who control their children may set their children up for blame, depression, nervousness, eating issues, and other psychological well-being conditions. One study also uncovered that parents who routinely use manipulation tactics on their children might increase the probability their children will also utilize manipulative behavior. Signs of manipulation in the parent-child relationship may incorporate making the child feel remorseful, absence of responsibility from a parent, making light of a child's achievements, and a should be associated with numerous aspects of the child's life.

People may also feel controlled if they are a piece of a friendship that has turned out to be dangerous. In manipulative friendships, one person might use the other to address their very own issues at the expense of their friend's. A manipulative friend may use blame or intimidation to concentrate favors, such as advancing cash, or they may connect with that friend when they need their very own enthusiastic needs met and may discover excuses when their friend has needs in the relationship.

EXAMPLES OF MANIPULATIVE BEHAVIOR

Sometimes, people may control others unconsciously, without being completely mindful of what they're doing, while others may effectively deal with strengthening their manipulation tactics. Some signs of manipulation include:

- Passive-aggressive behavior
- Verifiable threats
- Dishonesty
- Retaining data
- Isolating a person from friends and family
- Gaslighting
- Verbal abuse

Use of sex to accomplish goals

As the motives behind manipulation can change from unconscious to malicious, it's imperative to identify the circumstances of the manipulation that is occurring. While severing things might be necessary for situations of abuse, a therapist may help other people figure out how to manage or go up against manipulative behavior from others.

Step by step instructions to DEAL WITH MANIPULATIVE PEOPLE

When manipulation becomes lethal, managing the behavior from others can be exhausting. Manipulation in the working environment has been shown to diminish execution, and manipulative behavior from friends and family can cause reality to seem questionable. If you believe you are being controlled in any relationship, it might be useful to:

Disengage. If someone is attempting to get a specific enthusiastic response from you, choose not to offer it to them. For instance, if a manipulative friend is known to compliment you before asking for exceeding support, don't play along—instead, answer affably and move the conversation along.

Be sure. Sometimes, manipulation may incorporate one person's attempts to cause another person to question their abilities, instinct, or even reality. If this happens, it might stick to your story; in any case, if this frequently occurs in a close relationship, it could be an excellent opportunity to leave.

Address the situation. Get out the manipulative behavior as it's going on. Maintaining the focus on how the other person's actions are influencing you instead of starting with an accusatory statement may also enable you to arrive at a resolution while emphasizing that their manipulative tactics won't take a shot at you.

Stay on-subject. When you call attention to a behavior that makes you feel controlled, the other person may attempt to limit the situation or tangle the case by raising other issues as a distraction. Keep in mind your central matter and stick to that.

Psychological manipulation

Mental control is a sort of social influence that intends to change the recognition or conduct of others through clever, deceptive, or even harsh strategies. By progressing just, the interests of the controller, frequently at the other's cost, such techniques could be viewed as exploitative, oppressive, mischievous, and deceptive.

Social influence isn't negative. For instance, specialists attempt to influence patients to change undesirable propensities. Social influence is innocuous when it regards the privilege of the influenced to acknowledge or dismiss it, and isn't unduly coercive. Contingent upon the specific circumstance and inspirations, social influence may establish naughty control.

Psychological Manipulation Techniques

You've presumably found out about manipulative brain science and how you can use it or even how it's more likely than not being used on you to get you to do things that other people need you to do. In any case, it's useful to know a portion of these mental control systems with the goal that you can either build up your protection instruments or clandestinely use them on other people (for their general good obviously).

Putting down the other person

Typically, if you put another person down verbally, it runs a danger of appearing to be a personal assault.

Which raises their harasses and won't demonstrate you in a great light - very little use if you're attempting to get them to accomplish something you need.

Be that as it may, humor brings down the obstructions. Except for some elective comics, jokes are entertaining and not typically awful.

If you can transform your potential put down into a joke, it will in any case work a similar way yet it won't leave the noticeable scars.

One way to do it is to put the joke into the third person: "Other people...", that sort of thing. At that point, if the other person still theories that it's truly gone for them, qualify it with a throwaway line, for example, "present organization excepted."

Use made-up facts

The web does this consistently. Adverts do as well. Those eight out ten cats whose proprietors favored a specific brand were a deliberately chosen pack of cats. By restricting the example size and cautiously expressing the question in a way that even a legislator would be desirous, they found the solution they set out to get.

A great many people won't question explanations of "reality" mainly if you use them sparingly and qualify them with something like "an overview I read about said...".

It's stunningly better if you have given occasion to feel doubts about the reality because seed has been planted in the other person's brain. A bit like the moon landings where a right estimated segment of the world question whether they at any point occurred. Regardless of whether they did or not - I imagine that a shuttle arrived as appeared however I'm more uncertain about who was in it or whether they endure the radiation and different nasties - the seeds of uncertainty have also been planted, if it was so natural back toward the finish of the 1960s why, with all our innovation enhancements, hasn't anybody returned. Not by any means, the Russians or the Chinese for some one-upmanship. Be that as it may, hello, I stray.

Alright, so moon landings don't influence the majority of us a significant part of the time. Be that as it may, we can use other alleged realities to help convince other people round in our mind and manipulate their musings shockingly effectively.

Make an illusion

You don't need to be David Copperfield or Criss Angel to do this. They go through many months rehearsing their "incomprehensible" stunts.

Instead, you can build up a great deal of supporting proof to enable you to demonstrate whatever it is you're attempting to manipulate.

Road tricksters use saps and patsies. Be that as it may, that takes a considerable amount of work and requires the assistance of other people.

CHAPTER TWO

Characteristics of Emotional & Psychological Abuse

Abuse isn't restricted to physical violence. While mental and passionate control may leave no noticeable imprints, the impacts of these types of damage can be similarly as genuine as physical injury. Abuse that does not influence the body can have more noteworthy long-haul outcomes than abuse that leaves scars, yet it tends to be significantly more difficult to perceive. Figuring out how to recognize the signs and impacts of abuse is the initial step to consummation and avoiding genuine mischief.

The indications of physical abuse can be anything but difficult to recognize, yet frequently go unnoticed. Wounds, cuts, and different sorts of physical injury are regular markers of aggressive behavior at home and ought to consistently be paid attention to. Victims of abusive behavior at home usually likewise experience mental and psychological mistreatment and may feel vulnerable and unfit to get away from their abusers. Sometimes victims even excuse their abuse, causing themselves to accept they "merit" to be abused out of the blue.

Local abuse isn't the main wellspring of mental or psychological mistreatment. The inhabitants of nursing homes, for instance, are now and then abused by their guardians. Deceptive guardians may take or endeavor to pick up the trust of the inhabitants for money related reward, forcing them into giving over their investment funds, benefits, or different types of pay.

To mentally control their victims, abusers pay heed to their victims' specific weaknesses, fears, and mental vulnerabilities. Abusers conceal their activities behind a grin, or by exhibiting them as essential or excused, to get their victims to bring down their watchman. By then again offering positive and negative fortification, abusers can make their victims mentally subject to them.

Using Manipulative Psychology for Self-Improvement

Manipulative Psychology is a fantastic asset to reinvent your mind for making progress in all that you do and to manage people who attempt to control you by identifying their mystery moves.

Learning this technique isn't difficult; it falls into place without any issues for successful and persuasive people.

Manipulative Psychology is the step by step process that instructs you to be energetic, sure, and a prevailing player in your calling just as your connections. It's a scientific methodology that sharpens your intuitive social aptitudes to make you a characteristic head in your group of friends.

It's a sure-way to make you very well-known and the most respected individual in your gathering. You will figure out how to end up an outgoing individual and a specialist at taking care of difficult people. You can utilize these plans to charm anyone into giving a positive response to you.

You can utilize these techniques to revamp your reasoning process and changing your activities and conduct as needs are. Success evades a great many people since they are excessively bashful or reluctant to attempt another venture or thought, so the essential step to change yourself is by controlling your thoughts. Your thoughts are the outlines to your success in the external world. You should, in this manner, dispose of every single negative thought that continually impede your development as a person by deleting all your innovative vitality. Perhaps the ideal ways of doing that are by first identifying every single negative feeling and thoughts, and after that confining yourself from them. Figure out how to disregard them, and they'll vanish without anyone else's input, to do that you should draw in yourself into some critical action of your advantage. Another way of disposing of negative thoughts is by supplanting them with positive attestations, for example, "I can" rather than "I can't."

One of the most dominant techniques of self-improvement through Manipulative Psychology is the process of Visualization. You should envision yourself having all the positive characteristics that you wish to secure. Your intuitive mind is enriched with the ability to transform your thoughts into actions. This is a powerful way of controlling your sub-cognizant mind into turning your fantasies into the real world.

You can utilize these techniques on others to get them to do anything you need them to. For example, you can use the intensity of representation; you can cause your customers to picture that the venture you are proposing is of massive significance and fundamental for their development and can get a positive response from them. If you are an Employer, at that point, you can utilize this technique to make your workers feel significant for their association and subsequently can inspire them to use their most extreme efficiency.

If you are a representative, then you can convince your manager into giving you a sensible compensation climb or advancement by utilizing the powerful abilities you can learn through Manipulative Psychology.

Manipulative Psychology utilizes the craft of deciphering non-verbal communication to make your character additionally speaking to other people. You can likewise use this learning to precisely identify your customer's current mindset and translate their feelings, for example, bothering, fatigue, outrage, certainty and so on and after that successfully convince them to give a positive response when they are in their most responsive mindset.

Manipulative Psychology can give you a front line over your rivals, support your deals, and give you instant success and notoriety that you merit.

How People Are Manipulated Emotionally and Why

Emotional or mental manipulation means to impact the conduct of another person by specific tactics which may not be clear to the manipulated or even to others. The goal may not be to change the behavior of the manipulated person yet additionally to make him persuaded that there is no other method to escape the circumstance or that his association with the manipulator is unavoidable. It is a form of abuse. However, it may not be as apparent as other forms. Emotional manipulation is emotional abuse, which could be related to other forms of violence, for example, physical and sexual abuse.

There is a difference between influence and emotional manipulation. Influence isn't coercive and regards the privilege of the person to pick and to acknowledge or reject the recommended conduct. In manipulation, it might appear to be externally that the person is permitted to choose. Be that as it may, under the shallow affectation of the opportunity of decision, there is an undercurrent of emotional intimidation.

The process of emotional manipulation includes two gatherings: the manipulator and the manipulated in the process of manipulation, which has its very own elements.

The Manipulator:

Manipulators lie on a range of different characters. Nonetheless, they are altogether portrayed by variation from the norm in personality. It is anything but difficult to identify the heartless, unfeeling, insensitive, and callous sociopath. Be that as it may, some other scattered personalities may utilize manipulation to endure their very own pathology and keep up their mental respectability. An emotionally needy person may look for his emotional needs by controlling others. The equivalent with narcissistic personality when somebody takes a stab at satisfying their desire for power, glory, vanity, and self-glorification by controlling others. The theatrical which is looking for consideration, guilty pleasure, the fulfillment of shallow emotional and sexual needs may utilize all their enticing and sensational misrepresentations to control others. Individuals with Borderline personality with their clamorous feelings and feeling of inward vacancy, emotional episodes, heedless undertakings, and carrying on will control others even by their aggression or self-hurt.

The manipulator attempts to control the manipulated to keep up his emotional or personal gains. A few manipulators can without much of a stretch shift their concentration, starting with one victim then onto the next. However, others my battle as far as possible to hold their victim under their paws.

The Manipulated:

Everyone can be effectively manipulated. This is consistent with some degree, although an astute mental case can threaten the least powerless by tactics of fear.

The most defenseless against manipulation are those quiet and tentative persons who need self-assurance. They are ordinarily scrupulous, accommodating, genuine, or now and then guileless. They might be desolate persons, damaged and looking for shelter in the hands of the stable manipulator. They may need confidence, with a profound feeling of guilt, which is scanning for discipline and an inclination that they should have the right to be rebuffed.

Indeed, even the individuals who can intellectualize their life quandaries may misdirect themselves by working their mind hard into the shrouded justifiable explanations behind the manipulator to act along these lines. They discover pardons for the culprit however they disregard reasons to liberate themselves from the hands of the manipulator. They appreciate intellectualizing their enduring as they find out confronting their defenselessness too excruciating to even think about living with.

The Manipulation Process:

Different tactics are utilized in the manipulation process. Some are unmistakable, and others are too inconspicuous even to consider exploring or too complex to think about analyzing.

1. Instillation of Guilt:

Guilt is a reliable negative spark. Manipulators know by experience that their victims can feel regretful effectively. They see that the victim even admits his deficiencies and apologizes and feels humiliated pointlessly. Continuously, they make the victim accepts they are bad enough, they couldn't care less enough, or they are narrow-minded, brutal, exploitative, and even parasitic. Much of the time, the manipulator has the majority of these highlights. The victim cannot usually look to see this isn't accurate because he/she has been customized into self-question, self-fault, and admiration of others together with the deterioration of self.

2. Disgracing:

A manipulator utilizes tactics to make the victim feels disgraceful, dishonorable, and lacking so that there will never be a way out. If the victim attempts to challenge a manipulator, the last makes the victim feels embarrassed by terrorizing, dread, guilt and self-question, with the allegation of the absence of capacity to do anything, lack of stamina, power or fearlessness. Mockery, jokes, criticism, and negative remarks, or even just dangers might be utilized. Here and there, the manipulator incites the victim into a demonstration of aggression out of disappointment and torment. This usually neglects to free the victim. Be that as it may, the manipulator would utilize such occurrence to make the victim feels further disgrace, disappointment, and guilt.

3. Gaining Sympathy:

The manipulator may play the job of the victim to gain sympathy and collaboration if other tactics fizzle. Summoning empathy, pity, and compassion from somebody who is scrupulous aren't difficult all things considered persons can not stand seeing somebody who is enduring or in torment. The manipulator continues regretting how unfortunate they are, how out of line things are, and how they are victims of such remorseless life.

4. Terrorizing:

Dangers might be dull or secretive. A scary look, overlooking the other person, articulation of anger or dissatisfaction are a portion of the creepy demonstrations. Some of the time, it is pretending rage and a blast of feeling which is utilized to threaten the person into accommodation. Dangers may go from outrageous conduct to demolish the economic wellbeing of the victim up to physical assaults and once in a while dangers to slaughter.

5. Temptation:

Sexual manipulation is utilized to give a misguided feeling of closeness and guarantee the obligation of the relationship. Emotional enticement by sweet talk, acclaim, and beguiling disposition can be immediately used to make the victims bring down their barriers and gain their trust. This is typically brief and unusual, and through such discontinuous encouraging feedback, the victim is guided into the round of manipulation.

6. Lying:

Lying is at the center of manipulation either by retention a significant measure of reality, overlooking some vital actualities, or creating false stories. The manipulator may misrepresent or limit certainties, cheat and hoodwink the victim and fabricate unbelievable picture of himself, his victim, and their relationship. Faking is another form of pragmatic lying. The manipulator may deny that he has done anything incorrectly purposefully or that he was uninformed of the impact on the victim or may put on a look of shock or anger. Obvious lying through denying "what you are discussing?" or professing to be distracted or confounded is some of the time utilized. Pretending disease or pain, fainting, or false fits might be used to gain sympathy and debilitate the protections of the victim.

7. Legitimization:

The manipulator may utilize different moves to clarify the explanations behind his conduct, which use the helplessness of the victim. If the victim is credulous or incapable of passing judgment on a contention, the manipulator may utilize a large number of the false notions of rationale to defeat his victim's counter-contentions. If the victim is ridden with guilt, disgrace, or brutal soul, the manipulator utilizes all contentions which claim to such vulnerabilities.

8. Disavowal:

The manipulator may gruffly deny any wrongdoing or decline to let it out or avoid talking about the subject by and large. He/she may take part in a meandering, unessential befuddling talk which may occupy the thoughtfulness regarding an entirely unexpected matter. Forswearing is different from lying if the person is unconscious incompletely or entirely of reality.

9. Anticipating the fault:

The manipulator may extend the responsibility on the victim, blaming him for his very own large number indecencies or in some cases charge others who have wronged him for the duration of his life and who made him what he is. The victim may feel either guilty, or he is put on edge to account for himself, or he may feel sympathy and distress for the manipulator.

10. Aggression:

The manipulator may fall back on genuine aggression and savagery to cause the victim to submit to his will, specifically if the victim is flimsier or disabled. This may leave an abrupt in a pretended upheaval of indignation or severe anger. Any reaction of a comparable sort from the victim is looked with progressively extreme aggression which might be later accused on the victim himself, or a manufactured ailment might be charged or just ascribed to the emotional issues the manipulator professes to confront.

Don't Be Psychologically Manipulated When Negotiating

Do you become mentally hindered when negotiating? Is it true that you are mindful that keen people do imbecilic things since they're mentally manipulated when negotiating? Do you realize how much mental control happens and how to prevent it from transpiring? If you'd like to protect yourself from ploys that can lead to mental talk in your negotiations, see what pursues.

The accompanying five points are a couple of reasons why a few people are energized when negotiating. Regard this understanding to prevent mental controls from being constrained upon you.

1. Lack of negotiation strategy: Anytime anybody goes into a negotiation without a strategy about how they'll potentially accomplish their goals, they enter the negotiation ill-equipped. Before going into any negotiation, set aside the effort to build up a strategy that can lead to achieving the purposes of the negotiation.

2. Lack of control: Know your leave points in a negotiation, what should trigger those points, and don't be manipulated by ending up sincerely attached to a position, or associated with the negotiation to the point that you can't exit. You can be drawn further into a negotiation, because of your enthusiasm to accomplish the goals of the negotiation. Realize when to stop and do as such at the point you've set.

3. Time as a factor: Be mindful of the pressures time places upon you in a negotiation. Continuously remember, the additional time you put resources into a negotiation, mentally, the more you'll end up engaged and need to see the negotiation to its decision. You might be spurred mentally to do as such, regardless of whether it implies you submit acts that are negative to your negotiation position.

4. Picture: In an ideal situation, you should want to consult in a domain that is helpful for your style and way of negotiating, and one in which you can be seen as persuasive. To the degree you're seen with love, you've just started to make a subliminal impression from which you can be in the direction of the negotiation.

5. Combativeness: When engaged in a negotiation, a few moderators enable their self-images to end upswelled. In doing as such, some fall into the snare of being manipulated by either thinking the best way to win is by crushing the other mediator. Along these lines, they ignore potential circumstances in which bargain may lie. Such contemplations can be invigorated by the conviction that they're not seen by the other consulted with the reverence they merited. In this way, they embrace an, "I'll demonstrate to you" attitude. Continuously remember the banality, "He who battles and flees, lives to battle one more day." Don't be caught by this mental predicament. This way, you'll dodge the likelihood of assisting your death.

A few issues happen when people are rationally occupied and bothered in a negotiation. One, they lose their capacity to be discerning and two, they hazard getting to be hushed into a practically entrancing perspective. To prevent from winding up rationally furious, and taking part in unreasonable conduct that doesn't bolster your negotiation position, be objective and intelligent when negotiating. Don't be attracted into the snares referenced previously... what's more, everything will be direct with the world. Remember, you're continually negotiating.

The Negotiation Tips Are,

• In negotiation, know with whom you're negotiating, how severely they need/need what you're offering, and evaluate their diligence to rough to what extent they may remain engaged in the negotiation to acquire their goals.

• When negotiating, consistently leave a psychological acknowledged secondary passage open on the off chance that you endure a psychological breakdown. If need be, escape through it. Don't turn into a mental slave to mental craziness.

• To keep away from mental situations, never become involved with a hissy fit, and neglect to execute your negotiation plan. Continuously endeavor to control your feelings.

CHAPTER THREE

How to Read Minds

Numerous people discover the act of reading minds very overwhelming; a large portion of these individuals give different notions when gotten some information about individuals who have such gifts. Any individual can pick up the capacity of how to read minds this isn't an act for exceptional people or for people who may approach the supernatural world the same number of may clarify the wonder. Reading minds is influenced by laws of attractions which are ever-present with us; laws of attraction figure out our identity, what we are, and even the future we hope to have. The subject on universal laws of attraction a prickly issue among people today; anyway, individual who favor one side to minimize effects of laws of attraction disregard the fact that this power impacts every single individual be it a kid or a grown-up. Each individual's character and lifestyle is controlled by issues they've needed to experience in different phases of their lives. People reason and act from feelings and sentiments bolted inside their intuitive mind. Anybody keen on learning how to read minds should as a matter of first importance comprehend fundamental ideas of how the mind works to produce results in its functions.

There are a significant number of books which have been written about the functions of the mind and how one can build up their minds to perform wanted acts. Accentuation on conceivable outcomes in anything an individual focus on to do is simply the essential impact of influencing any development act. Reading books and other persuasive articles are the reason for which the mind makes conviction frameworks towards what an individual want. It is imperative to read books and articles which are written by great respectable journalists. Anybody keen on influencing any self-development act ought to know about the fact that arriving at an ideal objective does not occur without any forethought and that they'll be steady in anything they focused on to do.

Universal laws of attraction help in affecting self-awareness acts; the subject on effects of universal laws of attraction make loads of buzz among individual today, anyway research has it that these powers work whether an individual knows or not. People look to get data about laws of attraction turn support on their side in that they learn and influence common powers to work for their bit of leeway.

Universal laws of attraction set premise under which specific mind abilities are influenced, for example, reading mind suggests the synchronization of body mind and soul so as to try to realize what another person might make of; people who've arrived at cutting edge phases of reading minds can tell slants radiated by a gathering of people in a given setting. Individuals who are keen on learning how to read minds should, above all else do investigate the subject before influencing any self-development act to this effect. Mind reading is an imperative procured ability and is of incredible assistance to any individual who might be keen on achievement in different parts of their lives.

Mind Control and Its Effects

WHAT IS MIND CONTROL?

Many knows this psychological disease, for example, brain washing, **menticide**, coercive influence, thought control or thought change, depends on the concept that the mind can be modified or controlled by mental procedures. Mind control is said to decrease it is subject's capacity to think basically or autonomously, to permit the presentation of new, undesirable considerations and thoughts into the subject's mind, just as to change his or her frames of mind, qualities, and beliefs. The concept of teaching was initially created during the 1950s by a government to disclose how to cause their kin to collaborate with them.

Let it out - at any rate once in your life; you've wanted to learn how to do mind control and control the thoughts of others.

Possibly you wanted your child to do the tasks without whimpering. Maybe you wanted your wife to change her mind about the costly buy you've been peering toward. Or in another word, you could be sitting in your ho-murmur office, putting in additional time while your colleagues skate by.

Consider the possibility that you could change everyone around you. Imagine a scenario where you realized how to do mind control in a secretive manner.

We're not talking about enormous superhuman forces. You're not going to stroll into work tomorrow and all of a sudden place everybody in a stupor, so they pursue your directions like mechanical fighters. We're not talking about brainwashing, either.

You don't need unforgiving strategies of dread and control to realize how to do mind control and persuade others to do your will. Also, you don't need heavenly powers. All you need is control of your mind and the capacity to understand the minds of others. When you learn how to have full control of these things, you can learn how to do mind control that will change your life.

The human mind is dubious business, however by continually honing your mind-control skills, you can learn how to break through to others' subconscious to reformat how they think and subsequently, how they act.

Knowing how to do mind control on others is an incredible aptitude. It might appear to be unreasonably scary for you to master; however, don't stress. All you need to do to turn into a mind-control master is get your foot into the entryway of other people's subconscious. Here's the ticket:

Show a demeanor of authority and control

To have the option to work your mind-control techniques, people need to listen to you. Do you believe they will listen to the introvert in the corner or the bashful person contracting by the watercooler? No. They need to admire people of authority. They offer regard to the individuals who appear to have everything in perfect order.

Why? It's straightforward - that is the thing that they need, as well. When they feel tremendous and captivated of you, they begin to drop the shield that watches their subconscious, which gives you a full section. Knowing how to break the reinforcement is vital to knowing how to do mind control.

Push catches

This doesn't mean you need to have people into a tantrum of fierceness over some hot political issue. It means understanding what is most important to people. Become acquainted with their motivations and interests. When you do, unpretentiously push those catches until you're controlling their thoughts.

If you have their trust, they will bite by bit open themselves to you without acknowledging it. It's then that they are helpless against your proposals and influence.

Appease

Another advantage of knowing what people's personal qualities and motivations are is deciding how to control their minds by assuaging them. This implies making clandestine references to issues or points they feel enthusiastic about

When they see that you share, understand, or value their thoughts or thoughts, they begin to feel like you're a compatriot. They will focus on that specific point, which gives you significantly more opportunity to break through the subconscious shield. To realize how to do mind control, you should welcome the craft of humoring people.

Exercise your entitlement to be quiet

Quietness is a ground-breaking thing, considerably more dominant than people figure it out. You unquestionably don't have any desire to be the tight-lipped party pooper in the gathering. However, you would like to be the person who realizes how to do mind control techniques by deliberately using the privilege to stay quiet.

How? When associated with a genuine or profound discussion with somebody, don't stumble over their words. Don't interfere. Don't begin talking when they stop. At minutes in the debate, be quiet. Sooner or later you'll need to state something obvious, however in those couple of moments of distress; they're probably going to fill the space with more words. The more they talk, the more damaged they become.

Every one of these techniques should enable you to sneak your way into a person's subconscious, making them accessible to your influence. When you realize how to do mind control, plainly you saddle a magnetic force.

Learn The Essence Of Mind Control

We are altogether given a mind to think, and we are entirely brought into the world with a similar capacity to use our mind. The mind is the most dominant of all power's humankind can ever understand. One can hoist or debase oneself by one's very own mind. The mind can turn into one's closest friend or the most exceedingly awful foe. The mind shifts into a friend to the person who has control over it and turns into an adversary for the person who is controlled by the mind.

Why is it important to control your mind? An open mind resembles a wild steed, which has a ton of energy and continues pursuing such a significant number of things, whereas a controlled mind resembles a prepared steed. Envision attempting to channel all your mental energy towards one assignment. You will carry out a responsibility/task better if all your mental energy is directed appropriately towards it.

With a meandering mind, a person can't focus on his/her work and regularly needs to confront severe conditions and weight at work. It isn't so much that we don't have the foggiest idea how to work, it's merely that we do not have the foggiest idea how to regain control on our mind.

The facts demonstrate that we people have a limited ability to focus. However, that does not imply that we can't control our mind and get it in the groove again. Following are steps that can help you towards mind control.

Tips on How to mind control

1. Identify thoughts which occupy you

One of the essential reasons why we are not ready to center or focus is a direct result of specific thoughts with which our mind is consistently pre-involved. Give yourself some time and identify those thoughts and record it. When you have registered it, contemplate internally that these thoughts are aggravating and hurtful to you. Enjoy the self-talk. When you do this as a practice, whenever comparative ideas come to you, you will start talking to yourself and expel those thoughts from your mind.

2. Know about yourself

How frequently have you perused a page or tuned in to a melody or gone by a street without acknowledging what you read/heard/saw? It occurs with a considerable lot of us. The best activity is to know about you consistently. Know about where you are, your main thing. Know about your breathing rate, and so forth. When you place this in practice, you won't just be in the present; however, will likewise improve your memory.

3. Toss out negative thoughts

If you had a battle with your boss/spouse or somebody said something which you didn't care for, at that point I would propose that you put to practice called "negative thoughts discarding." Do this. Close your eyes and visualize the person for whom you have negative thoughts. When you see the person, start talking with that person. Disclose to him/her your position and examine with that person. Visualize the whole grouping of occasions and towards the end disclose to yourself that, presently you have stood up the entirety of your anger/negativity and that you will never allow this to anger/negativity bother you.

4. Don't overstress yourself

With so a large number heaping up today thus much work to do stress will undoubtedly occur. Stress influences your body, yet in addition to your mind. With stress, your mind stops to work and can't organize. When you lose control over the need in your life, you never again have control over your mind. Therefore, you will at times feel that a few assignments are significant than others, and the next moment you alter your perspective and something different ends up vital. This happens because you are not ready to choose from. Peruse this section on Tips for Stress Management

5. Reflect

As sustenance is to the body, meditation is to the mind. Meditation re-empowers you as well as causes you to regain control over your mind. Close your eyes and figure out how to unwind. Once in the loosened upstate, visualize an book. When the representation is clear, start focusing on that object. Focus on what it looks like, and it is shading, its shape, every one of its highlights, and so on. From the start, this activity is challenging, yet with the time, you will ace it. I am highly involved with composing a 10-minute meditation control.

How to Mind Control - Powerful Techniques for Influencing People

The learning of how to mind control gives you control over yourself, over others, and any social situation. You can cause anyone to do what you need, provided that you realize how to influence people.

The techniques that I will demonstrate to you here are both simple to use and effective. You can apply them to any person. Besides, they are superbly protected to use. You can readily apply them to your child if the individual in question is being difficult about doing schoolwork or going to class.

Here is the way to mind control using a variety of useful techniques.

Make the person feel indebted to you.

Anyone who does not understand how to mind control can use this simple technique. You have presumably used it ordinarily without realizing its capacity. You should highlight why you have had the right to get what you need from this person. You can readily remind an old friend how you have helped him before. A mother can easily say to her child, "I am your mother. I love you so much, and I have done as such much for you. Doing this (the thing that you need) will make me feel glad."

The way to progress is to use ground-breaking words, for example, "love" and "glad" in the instance above. It is additionally essential to highlight the results of the positive effect to make the suggestion all the more dominant.

Try not to allow the person to state "no."

This is another effortless technique you can use. One of the most common examples of its use is to ask someone for what good reason he loves you instead of asking him whether he loves you.

This is a ground-breaking psychological stimulus. You are pointing the person's mind into the direction you desire. He is never again pondering between "yes" or "no." This stage has been automatically skipped. In turn, the person is bound to do what you need.

Another application of these techniques is to ask someone you need some help from, "How might you help me" instead of "Would you be able to support me?" Similarly, "What would we be able to do" is more dominant than "Would we be able to accomplish something?"

Since you realize how to mind control using this technique, you will perceive what number of applications it has in life and how useful it can be for influencing anyone.

Communicate non-verbally to make a ground-breaking subconscious influence.

This might sound a bit odd. However, you will see in only a second that it is effortless. Communicating subconsciously alludes to using facial expressions, signals, manner of speaking, and other non-verbal types of communication for getting a message over.

For instance, when you state to someone that you feel beautiful; however, you look crushed, it is apparent that you are not exceptional. You can readily use this type of communication to influence others.

Perhaps the most straightforward ways are to state, "Fine, I concur," and make a grumpy face.

You can readily begin crying if you realize how to mind control astonishingly. The impact in the two cases will be similar. The other person will be shaken, and he will be prepared to do what you need or possibly prepared to negotiate.

The above example is elementary, yet you can readily develop this basis. For example, you can promptly feel someone stupid for refusing to do what you need by saying, "Do what you need" and giving him a hideous or mocking smile.

Demonstrate the benefits the person will get from doing what you need.

This is another simple and effective psychological technique. It is generally used in deals. However, you can readily apply it on anyone, provided that you realize how to mind control.

The way to progress is to make the person feel that he needs to make this move and that you are an impartial observer. Make sure to link these benefits to the person's needs and qualities.

For instance, if you would prefer not to walk the canine on a rainy morning, you can readily ask your flat mate, who has quite recently parted ways with his girlfriend, to do it by saying that he might meet a superb girl walking her pooch.

You have quite recently figured out how to mind control in different ways. Continue expanding your insight to turn out to be considerably increasingly influential.

POWERFUL MIND CONTROL

You likely think it is incomprehensible. However, you can learn and ace different mind control techniques.

These are incredible assets for making others do what you need them to. There is a lot of ways wherein you can be a decent controller, yet it is ideal for concentrating on the best ones. Get familiar with the best mind control techniques.

Love bombing may sound strange. However, it is a fundamental and effective method of control. It is one of the mind control techniques that have been verified to work.

As the name proposes, your errand is to make the person you need to control like you and feel good around you through making him feel loved. There are different stages that this technique includes.

You need to begin by complimenting the person, with the goal that he promptly prefers you.

At that point, you can center ob building compassion in your relationship. This is best done by sharing your feelings and privileged insights (not the genuine ones, however). You must be on a similar wavelength as the person. Make him feel that you like very similar things and offer the same thoughts.

The physical contact is critical for the accomplishment of this one of the mind control techniques. You can promptly give the person a warm embrace when he needs it or holds his hand during an intense minute.

Given that you are doing everything effectively, the person you need to control will consider you family. This will enable you to impact him effectively. This person will be set up to take care of you thoroughly.

Rejection of old values is another of the active mind control techniques. The key objective here is to change the way to think about the person, with the goal that you can make him increasingly accommodating to your recommendations.

You need to concentrate on repudiating the current values of the person. This requires significant investment and exertion. However, you will achieve it with steadiness.

You need to begin with repudiating the convictions of the person. This can be effectively done through addressing. Along these lines, the person will feel that he has arrived at the resolution-independent from anyone else.

At that point, you can work on the absolute rejection of old values. The ideal way to achieve achievement is to supplant them with new ones.

For instance, if a person feels that what is essential most is having a great time, you can promptly persuade him that what makes a difference the most is kinship (and your fellowship, specifically).

When you have changed the person utilizing this one of the mind control techniques, you can concentrate on making him do what you need. Utilize the rejection of the old values and the acknowledgment of new ones as your weapons.

Covert hypnosis is another of the mind control techniques that work splendidly. It is more clear than the other two, although it includes the utilization of an assortment of sub-techniques.

The favorable principle position of utilizing this method is that you can apply it on anyone, even outsiders, expertly, and rapidly.

Covert hypnosis is accomplished throughout a customary discussion. It has three principal stages - building rapport with the subject, arriving at his subconscious mind and making subliminal messages.

You can utilize both love bombing and the rejection of old values as a feature of this method. The first of the mind control techniques are useful for building rapport, making the subject like you.

You can promptly utilize the physical touch marvelously for arriving at the subconscious mind of the subject too.

The value rejection of mind control techniques can be utilized for making disarray. This can be especially effective for turning off the essential mind and impacting the subconscious one.

When the person is in the condition of daze, you can promptly make the recommendations, subliminal messages. Now you need to state what you need the other person to do. If you are conversing with a pretty young lady that you need to ask out, you need to report, "Go out with me." She will.

These mind control techniques have been verified to work. You should commit time and exertion to ace them. Continue learning and rehearsing to cause others to do what you need them to.

CHAPTER FOUR

EMOTIONAL-BEHAVIORAL PATTERNS

Passionate behavioral conduct standards show up, on its substance, to avoid some critical pieces of human brain science. Where are the mental, the exuberant, and explicitly the physical and resolutions? Enthusiastic standards of conduct seem to propose some inclination or feeling that fittings honestly into a show or some similarity thereof and depicts some foreseen line of horrid spreading out, sounding careless and detrimental.

No issues as yet, in our perception of passionate personal conduct standards. In any case, there is a spot for instinct, for essentialness, similarly concerning the human and compelling. Although these examples are not a distinguishing strength in social brain research, our view of human conduct, both interior and outside, drives us, sensibly soon, to watch the monotonous thought of people. Apparently, outward appearances, genuine sign, speed of advancement, game plan of conduct, standard of direct imparting regards and diversions, tendencies, inclinations, and level of care are adequate to make them heave our arms with frustration: how, how, and by strategies for what is the human-animal separated from any being whose mindfulness emanates from and is overpowered by the base chakras of dread, survival, having a spot, and verifying?

By and large, by a full edge, individuals live their lives in a condition of emergency, under principles of survival, dreading the most perceptibly horrendous, foreseeing failure, yearning for awful violence, dejection, shortage, imagining the assaults of time, the start of torment, calamity, and frustration - in this way, believing a fiasco of life a million times more awful than what will, almost certainly, ever transpire.

What are we to make of this? Do we genuinely live in a condition of franticness anything like the one we dread? Is our state of fear in any way proportional to the hazard introduced? Does our level of strain in any position address a better than average response to what may happen us?

The dread of poverty, I have seen, as a rule, is logically dominating in people who approach more than standard resources. The terror of death in the people who are not using any means wiped out, also in primary condition. The dread of sadness (in rank, for example) logically present in the people who show up, on its substance, progressively engaging prospects for companionship. What do we make of this? Dread assumes the presence of a craze, loss of movement, and daze, among various emotions, stows away in terror, franticness, threatening, and hesitance, and is pitifully disguised in pressure, shakiness, and uneasiness. People today are shy, disturbed, contracted, disrupted, tense, and uneasy, which are, generally, signs of dread.

The past psychotherapist, by and by writer, and powerful and social onlooker, Stephanie Dowrick, points out that the dread of death is a bit of the child's underlying contribution, as demonstrated by Melanie Klein. Dowrick continues to state:

The very beginning woven stories to ensure 'somethings.' Heaven, revival, the hover past... let me know through my body that I am alive because it is without a doubt my body, which will be unequivocally dead.

She continues to discuss sex, drinks at the bar, and human contact as approaches to keep up a critical, good ways from dread, melancholy, sentiments of unlovableness, and give up... in any case, a conclusive is the evasion of death. Fear of death covers a progressively significant worry, as I have elucidated already:

To live - to truly live - there is uncommonly only one dread to endure. Just one uncertainty since it is the one which incorporates all the others. That is the dread of death. Inside this persevering, apprehension is our refusal of life, our evasion of experience, our nonattendance of strength throughout everyday life, and finally, our dread of life. Fear of death is dread of life, and now you sense what the voyage of self-revelation has been about. It is the shedding of worry as our obsession with survival, our dread of not existing, our tendency to rise out of the ground of being and recognize ourselves as (and here is the unimaginable reason for the choice) our individual, separate Self or as the certifiable Self.

The mechanics of the passionate personal conduct standards are as incredible and evident as they are prescriptive and restricting... we dread our demise; we dread our dread - yet our most significant concern is our dread of life:

Enthusiastic standards of conduct are the modified ways wherein we respond to life-customized because that is how we dodge risk and shakiness. We dread! We dread unanticipated. We dread powerlessness. See someone walking around any new condition, since it's more straightforward to watch others - anyway better still look at yourself. You plan what you will say, how you act, and how you will relate. You have an accumulation of likelihood and prosperity. You respond inside the parameters of these predicted conditions and your rehearsed "responses."

Life is so nailed down for an enormous part of us, and there is no space for the shocking, the unconstrained - for the launch of the blessed. Concerning "the growing sacred reality," the creator Ken Carey forms:

Dread has a little undertaking to do in Creation. It fills in as a notice framework, instructing each animal concerning conduct that may cause usual mischief. Its responsibility is to verify the physical body. It was never expected to rouse people. Where dread is viewed as a source motivation, perception diminishes... The Fall happened when human thought went to fear...

We have connected at a clear truth: the dread that underlies our selling-out our humankind and building up our lives through intentional, passionate conduct designing was never wanted to be our strategy for living, hiding behind the sequentially misinformed prerequisite for affirmation, feeling "safe" through controlling the life-control.

The dread of death is dread of offering up to Infinity.

Make sense of how to offer up, to exist at Infinity while alive, and dread of death separates.

The dread of death is dread of the Unknown.

Passionate behavioral conduct standards show up, on its substance, to avoid some critical pieces of human brain science. Where are the mental, the exuberant, and explicitly the physical and resolutions? Enthusiastic standards of conduct seem to propose some inclination or feeling that fittings honestly into a show or some similarity thereof and depicts some foreseen line of horrid spreading out, sounding careless and detrimental.

No issues as yet, in our perception of passionate personal conduct standards. In any case, there is a spot for instinct, for essentialness, similarly concerning the human and compelling. Although these examples are not a distinguishing strength in social brain research, our view of human conduct, both interior and outside, drives us, sensibly soon, to watch the monotonous thought of people. Apparently, outward appearances, genuine sign, speed of advancement, game plan of conduct, standard of direct imparting regards and diversions, tendencies, inclinations, and level of care are adequate to make them heave our arms with frustration: how, how, and by strategies for what is the human-animal separated from any being whose mindfulness emanates from and is overpowered by the base chakras of dread, survival, having a spot, and verifying?

By and large, by a full edge, individuals live their lives in a condition of emergency, under principles of survival, dreading the most perceptibly horrendous, foreseeing failure, yearning for awful violence, dejection, shortage, imagining the assaults of time, the start of torment, calamity, and frustration - in this way, believing a fiasco of life a million times more awful than what will, almost certainly, ever transpire.

What are we to make of this? Do we genuinely live in a condition of franticness anything like the one we dread? Is our state of fear in any way proportional to the hazard introduced? Does our level of strain in any position address a better than average response to what may happen us?

The dread of poverty, I have seen, as a rule, is logically dominating in people who approach more than standard resources. The terror of death in the people who are not using any means wiped out, also in primary condition. The dread of sadness (in rank, for example) logically present in the people who show up, on its substance, progressively engaging prospects for companionship. What do we make of this? Dread assumes the presence of a craze, loss of movement, and daze, among various emotions, stows away in terror, franticness, threatening, and hesitance, and is pitifully disguised in pressure, shakiness, and uneasiness. People today are shy, disturbed, contracted, disrupted, tense, and uneasy, which are, generally, signs of dread.

The past psychotherapist, by and by writer, and powerful and social onlooker, Stephanie Dowrick, points out that the dread of death is a bit of the child's underlying contribution, as demonstrated by Melanie Klein. Dowrick continues to state:

The very beginning woven stories to ensure 'somethings.' Heaven, revival, the hover past... let me know through my body that I am alive because it is without a doubt my body, which will be unequivocally dead.

She continues to discuss sex, drinks at the bar, and human contact as approaches to keep up a critical, good ways from dread, melancholy, sentiments of unlovableness, and give up... in any case, a conclusive is the evasion of death. Fear of death covers a progressively significant worry, as I have elucidated already:

To live - to truly live - there is uncommonly only one dread to endure. Just one uncertainty since it is the one which incorporates all the others. That is the dread of death. Inside this persevering, apprehension is our refusal of life, our evasion of experience, our nonattendance of strength throughout everyday life, and finally, our dread of life. Fear of death is dread of life, and now you sense what the voyage of self-revelation has been about. It is the shedding of worry as our obsession with survival, our dread of not existing, our tendency to rise out of the ground of being and recognize ourselves as (and here is the unimaginable reason for the choice) our individual, separate Self or as the certifiable Self.

The mechanics of the passionate personal conduct standards are as incredible and evident as they are prescriptive and restricting... we dread our demise; we dread our dread - yet our most significant concern is our dread of life:

Enthusiastic standards of conduct are the modified ways wherein we respond to life-customized because that is how we dodge risk and shakiness. We dread! We dread unanticipated. We dread powerlessness. See someone walking around any new condition, since it's more straightforward to watch others - anyway better still look at yourself. You plan what you will say, how you act, and how you will relate. You have an accumulation of likelihood and prosperity. You respond inside the parameters of these predicted conditions and your rehearsed "responses."

Life is so nailed down for an enormous part of us, and there is no space for the shocking, the unconstrained - for the launch of the blessed. Concerning "the growing sacred reality," the creator Ken Carey forms:

Dread has a little undertaking to do in Creation. It fills in as a notice framework, instructing each animal concerning conduct that may cause usual mischief. Its responsibility is to verify the physical body. It was never expected to rouse people. Where dread is viewed as a source motivation, perception diminishes... The Fall happened when human thought went to fear...

We have connected at a clear truth: the dread that underlies our selling-out our humankind and building up our lives through intentional, passionate conduct designing was never wanted to be our strategy for living, hiding behind the sequentially misinformed prerequisite for affirmation, feeling "safe" through controlling the life-control.

The dread of death is dread of offering up to Infinity.

Make sense of how to offer up, to exist at Infinity while alive, and dread of death separates.

The dread of death is dread of the Unknown.

How to Read People

Diving deep into the benefits and the moral issues identifying with reading the minds of other people can without much of a stretch be expelled on the short ground that it's anything but a dynamic thought. As it were, it is genuine likewise as a result of the very aggressive and hardhearted circumstance that wins in each field. Reading people's minds presents numerous advantages. It is undoubtedly conceivable additionally. However, the techniques must be polished reliably with the goal that your decisions are close immaculate. A portion of the methods is talked about here.

By watching the body language and eye movements of a person, you can find out what the person is thinking. Reading the sign of the body language and eye movements is an extraordinary skill, and if it is aced, you can accomplish a lot of things. A few people appear to have this skill usually yet a large number of us don't focus on the sign that exudes from other people through these things. If you need to obtain this skill, you should begin giving more consideration to these perspectives.

- An incredible method to read the minds of people is to watch their eye movements. Specialists have discovered that if a person looks upward and to one side, the individual is making attempts to make an image. If a person looks upward and to one side, you can understand that the individual in question is making attempts to recall a specific image.

Another point is that anxious people or the individuals who talk falsehoods won't take a gander at your eyes straightforwardly. If the person is modest or meek, and still, at the end of the day, you can not anticipate that the person should take a gander at you legitimately.

Then again, certain people keep their eye contact for a more drawn out term. Same is the situation with sweethearts. By viewing the outward appearances likewise, you can make out what is fermenting in the minds of people.

- If somebody is attempting to draw near to you, they will react emphatically when you draw nearer to them. They will remain where they are or will try to come somewhat closer. If they don't savor you drawing closer to them, they will withdraw a little or move away from the scene.

- While talking with a person, if the person concurs with you, the knees will be pointed towards you. In actuality, if the knees are gotten some distance from you, you can presume that whatever you state isn't adequate to them.

So also, apprehensive or fretful people continue shifting their weight or moving their feet. If you watch a person sitting with his or her legs crossed, you can undoubtedly make out that an individual is a nice person.

- The head position will likewise assist you in determining what people think. Tilted heads demonstrate that they have compassion toward you. A tilted leader with a grin on the face shows that the individual in question is an energetic person, or it can even be deciphered as an indication of being a tease. If the person brings down the head while talking, you can make sure that the individual in question is attempting to conceal something.

- Some people will attempt to reflect your conduct. This demonstrates they are keen on you and are trying to make an association with you. To test this, you can make a couple of changes your conduct, and if they additionally attempt to mirror these changes, you can make sure that you particularly inspire them.

- You ought to likewise watch the movement of arms to read a person's mind. If the person creases or crosses his or her arms around the chest, they are attempting to shield themselves from others' persuasions. If they keep their feet more extensive with such crossed arms, these people are showing their sturdiness. If the hands are retained on the hips, you can presume that they are getting restless. By keeping their arms behind, they are demonstrating that they are not unwilling to exchanges.

You ought not to become fixated on this part of reading others. If you are over-ardent, others will find out that you are attempting to find out what they think or endeavoring to read them. They will end up being somewhat unbending with you. This may ruin your association with people. Along these lines, you ought to embrace an unobtrusive methodology while you attempt to read people.

Read People Instantly - The Power of Persuasion

Would you like to read people's mind? I mean, would you like to realize how to understand people instantly? Numerous scientists and specialists state that it is genuinely impossible to read the mind of people and understand them by merely looking at them. They are right; you will never realize that person except if you conversed with him a great deal, go with him as a rule, and spent time with him.

In marketing and deals, it is essential that you can read people instantly because you are not going to meet only one person for every day. You will never go anyplace by that. There is one powerful tool that will enable you to read people instantly and instantly; you can get what you need. The tool I'm saying here is not a thing, it is in you, and you need to create it. This is the power and art of persuasion that is hidden in you.

All of us has a hidden persuasion. You need to exercise and train yourselves on the most proficient method to utilize them, especially reading people. Reading people instantly is not excessively straightforward, but instead, with the power of persuasion, you will figure out how to read people immediately. You will discover that persuasive technique in here.

The power of persuasion can genuinely enable you to pull out something from the princely, and that is how you are going to read and understand them. There are different ways on how you can read people; however, just this art of persuasion that you can read them instantly. Like for instance, you can read people through their body language. You will honestly know if that person is interested in you by his body language.

Another model that you can read people; however, just these powers of persuasion, you can pull them out instantly are the facial expression and eye movement. Only even the facial expression, you can read a great deal from that. Your persuasion technique will enable you to determine what's with that expression, did they understand you, and do they believe in you or trust you? Your persuasion and how you induce people will respond to that question instantly.

Practice makes immaculate, right? I appeared to you in the passages on how persuasion can enable you to read people instantly, yet how are you going to free this persuasion that is hidden inside of you?

Mind Reading Technique For You to Try

A mind-reading technique is to be utilized not only to persuade a person that you can genuinely peruse minds. It is additionally to be used to verify that you are doing it effectively. Other than that, one ought to know about it so he won't risk being deluded by other people or persuaded to complete a specific assignment. Although the exactness of mind reading is questionable, it is annoying witness to by numerous that however you prevail with regards to doing it, you can't dispose of the risk that the person would get you. There are different techniques which a person may utilize contingent upon his inclination.

Here is a straightforward case of a mind-reading technique. By investigating the eyes of somebody, a person may realize what that person is thinking or if he is coming clean. In an example, you met a person or a young lady, and you questioned that person. If the person's eyes look into, he is in all probability thinking of the potential answers to your questions. He does this by making in your mind a picture or a thing would fill in as an answer to your question. Visual people are how these people, who give visible words which would remain as answers to the question, are called. If then again, the person's eyes look from side to side; he is most likely an auditory person. A hearing person, in contrast with the visual person, utilizes audible words to react to the question. He summons up a combination of sounds in his mind before he will identify the answer. Sensation persons who are known for utilizing sensation words would have their eyes looking down while perceiving out a specific inclination or sensation which has an association with the question. Another strategy is put into thought the person's (both the person asking and the person who reacts) inspiration and his or her next activity.

The said mind-reading technique for an assortment of people could be useful. If the person experiences a visual, auditory, or sensation person, he may add to his strategy the utilization of words which are added now and again misused by the person whom he is conversing with. By doing this, you will create the impact that both of you share a few similitudes and would most likely form affinity. Getting into the mind of a person would likewise compensate you with the information of what sort of person you are to that person. A few methodologies are intended to accomplish that. However, you ought to be set up to realize what the person in question considers you. On account of performers, however, their strategy depends more on the introduction. If they did not arrange their tricks in such a way, that would delight the group of spectators, and the observers would pitifully get the stunt. So for entertainers, their strategy is to rehearse, practice well, and convey their tricks convincingly. Concerning the individuals who are not entertainers, similar principles additionally apply. If they practiced their strategy routinely, they would be increasingly productive when playing out the technique.

CHAPTER FIVE

How to Control People Using Hypnosis

Figuring out how to control people utilizing hypnosis is something that the vast majority compare with having the option to make your companion stroll around like a chicken. While something like this is conceivable, it is only a hint of something more substantial as far as the power and down to earth uses that hypnotism holds. This FAQ is intended to answer probably the most widely recognized question about this class of hypnosis.

Who can be controlled utilizing hypnotism? - Hypnosis procedures can control absolutely anybody. Different people have different degrees of receptivity, yet everyone on the substance of the earth is defenseless to hypnotism.

Could a person use hypnosis to cause someone to accomplish something they typically wouldn't do? - Yes, however not really on the first attempt, or second or third so far as that is concerned. Hypnotism works by first making them vulnerable to your suggestion and after that recommending it.

That is why you can't directly go up to anyone and state, "Hello, bark like a canine." Because you initially need to make their mind helpless to the suggestion so it would appear to be typical for them to do it when you state it. If, for instance, you attempted to use hypnosis to cause someone to victimize a bank (God disallow), it would take days, weeks or long stretches of constant tweaking to at last get them to proceed with it. You couldn't merely cause them to do it from the very beginning, and you would need to make a few little changes in their speculation before they would consider ransacking a bank "ordinary."

What is a portion of the different sorts of hypnosis? - There are a wide range of varieties, beyond any reasonable amount to list every one of them here, yet the most broadly used are NLP (Neuro-Linguistics Programming), conventional hypnosis (where they essentially simply turn out and guide you), and conversational hypnosis (accepted by a large portion of the hypnotism network to be the most potent type of hypnotism for it's adequacy, speedy outcomes and application to practically any ordinary circumstance).

What is conversational hypnosis? - Conversational hypnosis is mesmerizing someone by methods for a characteristic yet coordinated conversation. Mostly, you go about as though you are having a typical discussion. However, you are organizing where it goes, bringing the person down different roads of idea and rationale. In the end, you will almost certainly take their considerations any place you need them to go, and by then you can start to make incognito suggestions to them. The thing is, they don't have any acquaintance with it's going on because the conversation feels so ordinary. This is why it is so powerful.

How does conversational hypnosis work? - There are three essential advances. Construct rapport, occupy, recommend. A few people say building rapport merely is getting the person to like you. However, it is hugely about getting in a state of harmony with another person so that everything done or said between you feels streaming and standard. Diversion is only that, taking the person's brain off what you need them to do. The last advance is proposing. When they are in an open state, you make your unobtrusive little suggestion, and if you did everything right, they acknowledge it.

You can contrast it with a fight; Building rapport resembles venturing into the ring with the other person. Diversion is the fakes and pokes you convey lose him gatekeeper, and suggestion echoes the right snare you toss to thump them out. If they are wide open and your hit grounds, BAM, they acknowledge the recommendation no questions inquired. Presently, obviously, with certain people you can end the battle in one hit, others may take two or three rounds, however, in the end, you will win out if you are doing it right. Additionally, the more confused or complicated the errand is, the more it will take for the suggestion to grab hold.

What are some commonsense uses for figuring out how to control people utilizing hypnosis? There is many you can do with this. Experiencing difficulty with the contrary sex? Using the powers of hypnotism would empower you to keep any person excited by whatever you need to state, embedding thoughts in their mind that make it unthinkable for them not to like you. Is it okay to say that you are a sales rep? Take a conversation where you need it to proceed to make it incomprehensible for the forthcoming customer to disapprove of whatever you are advertising — being harassed at school or work? Make the considerable person down and use your powers of suggestion to make him never trouble you again. The potential outcomes are close boundless.

Well I trust this has addressed a portion of your questions and provoked your advantage a smidgen about this astonishing art. I truly would prescribe facilitating your insight into hypnosis.it is the fact that it is fun; it's amazingly gainful in virtually every aspect of life.

Have some good times and Success in the entirety of Your Endeavors,

The Secret Tricks to Read People's Thoughts

Perhaps the best riddle of humankind is finding the key to how to peruse people's minds. If you could examine people's considerations, you could know precisely what someone else is thinking. The intensity of mind-reading stunts and techniques truly lies in your capacity by the way you are reading the conduct and signals that the other person gives you. Here are the mystery approaches to peruse people's contemplations through body language. When you realize what a person is supposing, you are in control of ground-breaking information that can enable you to lead interaction to support you.

Reading body language is fun and straightforward. The vast majority of us don't do this intentionally, so we neglect to perceive precisely what an extraordinary mind-reading technique it is. Here is the thing to watch out for to kick you off:

* If they are confronting you, they are tuning in and focusing on you. If they are dismissed, they are not centered around you. If they are shaking side to side, they are eager and need to end the conversation. A turned back is a sign of purposely disregarding or evading someone.

* When someone backs up, on a subliminal level they feel undermined and are withdrawing from you. If someone is step by step moving towards you, they are keen on you or what you are stating.

* Pointing their knees or their feet towards you is an all-inclusive sign they are in concurrence with you, they are adjusting their stance to yours.

* If they start to emulate your body language, that is a sign that you are driving the discussion.

* - Crossed arms are a sign of preventiveness or hatred, and the exemption is when the thumbs are unmistakable and pointing upwards, that implies they are feeling disengaged however genial.

* If their hands are confronting you with open palms, at that point they are accessible/responsive to what you are stating.

* If eyes look upward to one side they are attempting to make a picture from nothing. They are effectively utilizing their creative mind, and this can be a sign that they are making up whatever they are disclosing to you. If their eyes look upwards to one side, they are attempting to recall a specific picture, get to a particular memory. These are only the standard rules, a few people, particularly the left-gave, have the contrary eye developments, so it's essential to get a pattern reading by convincing them to recall something that you know occurred

The more significant part of these things we will feel during our interactions. Without giving mindful consideration, we will begin to sense when a person is getting to be cautious and at precisely that point see their shut body language. Figuring out how to focus on your emotions is a simple method to begin winding up increasingly mindful of what the body language of others is letting you know.

Beside sociopaths and ongoing liars, double-dealing is unpleasant. When we are worried, blood flow is organized to the essential organs and occupied away from the limits. If someone is lying, they are in all respects prone to have cold hands. This pressure will likewise make the person progressively jittery in light of an uproarious clamor or some other alarm. In any case, recollect, stress does not suggest trickery.

Eye contact when we are lying isn't healthy, however, it tends to be constrained. If a person begins looking that feels off, at that point, they are likely calculating something obscure.

How a person is thinking will be reflected in the words they use and the inquiries they pose. Someone who likes to discuss social circumstances and connections is someone who is centered around interpersonal relationships and will react much better to interactions that join those components. Relationships depend on feelings, and these people will be influenced more by passionate contentions than coherent ones.

By focusing on every one of the signs a person is accidentally emitting, you will appear to peruse their mind. These techniques will give you a consciousness of what others are imagining that you may even begin to astonish yourself with your exactness. The vast majority are so centered around what they are going to state straightaway or what they ask for from an interaction that they are just occupying an exceptionally modest quantity of their attention to the next person. When we center our complete consideration around what the other person is doing and saying, we increase immense understanding into what they are thinking, however, how they believe.

How to Identify a Manipulator

Manipulators are regular people we trust and that we consider as close-ones. We get things done for them because of that cozy relationship. Be that as it may, is that relationship truly as close as you might suspect it seems to be? Infrequently, it's great to make a stride back and reconsider the companions that you need to check whether they fit the personality type of a manipulative individual While you can at present be companions with a manipulator, you should be cautious when they are mentioning things from you.

Sensible Versus Emotional Arguments

Legitimate arguments bode well to a great many people because there is identifiable and robust proof to help that argument. When I state that the Earth rotates around the sun, people will accept that announcement because there is scientific proof to support that guarantee. Passionate discussions are the essential ammo for manipulators. Emotional arguments are those cases that are not founded on objective criteria, but instead dependent on sentiments and feelings. An example of this is if I needed you to get me a PC because you love me, isn't that so? The manipulator's solicitations, supports, or needs usually don't have any coherent reasoning behind them because they are narrowly minded in nature. The manipulator realizes that they can't use sound arguments to convince you to do what they need, so they switch over to passionate arguments to control their justification. This is the first approach to identify a manipulative individual. Their rationale will consistently be imperfect, and heated arguments will always uphold their reasoning.

The Four Tactics that Manipulators Use

Speaking to your love. The manipulator will interest your relationship with them to impact you. They will refer to their relationship with you as a spine of getting you to do what they need. They will use words, for example, "trust," "love," and "us."

Speaking to your feeling of blame. The manipulator will endeavor to impact you by making you feel very regretful for declining their solicitation. A run of the mill line is, "Well if you truly thought about me, you would do this."

Terrorizing. The manipulator may lose control at your refusal to complete some help for them, and they will take a stab at utilizing a forceful and threatening way to deal with the power you to submit out of dread.

Counterfeit Flattery. The manipulator will give you excessive and, regularly underserved, compliments with an end goal to "flatter you" for the support that will come straightaway. This is a type of self-image stroking that brings down your watchman for intelligent reasoning and makes supports all the more simple to surrender to.

Is Your Friend Manipulating You?

You're feeling ambiguous disdain, yet you don't know why. Your friend appears to solicit more from you, anticipate a higher amount of you than you're willing to give. You're feeling guilty for not ceding to your friend's solicitation. You wind up asking why you're accomplishing something when you genuinely don't have any desire to. If thus, perhaps you're being controlled.

Typically manipulators need to have power and control or attention and compassion more than their offer. They presumably saw you were in a powerless circumstance new around the local area, feeling uncertain or timid. Perhaps you're battling with confidence issues of your own. That is when they move in to dominate.

It's challenging to identify manipulative behavior because there are such huge numbers of approaches to misuse another person, and some of them are exceptionally unobtrusive. Manipulators slip into a circumstance and apply more control increasingly after some time, and you may not see until it's gotten way crazy. The key is to be alert.

Ask yourself how they profit by their behavior. When their motivation isn't to your most significant advantage, you have fallen prey to a Master Manipulator.

How might you identify and deal with a Master Manipulator? Here are a few models:

MM: I don't perceive how you can go on your camping trip and leave me to deal with this project independent from anyone else.

You: I have arranged this trip for quite a while, and you thought about it. I have just contributed my part to the project.

The MM is attempting to make you feel guilty, or more terrible, trying to get you to remain at home and do his work on the project for him.

MM: Jennifer disclosed to me she figured you weren't generally contributing as a lot to the project as other individuals.

You: I trust you revealed to her that I had done my part. However, I can't generally be worried about what Jennifer thinks.

The NN is attempting to utilize an outsider to get you to do what the NN himself needs.

NN: I'm anxious that this project won't turn out well, and my reputation is hanging in the balance. I genuinely feel debilitated with stress, and you know how my circulatory strain is.

You: My reputation is hanging in the balance as well, which is why I've prepared and done my part. Presently it's your turn to do your part.

The NN, in every case, needs more careful attention than any other individual and will utilize blame to get the attention he needs.

NN: Okay, go on your camping trip while I remain at home working all end of the week on the project.

You: Great. I'm happy you'll have room schedule-wise to work on it. See you when I get back.

The NN attempted one final time to get you to feel guilty, and played the saint. In any case, you challenged his blustering, held your ground, and cut him off. Bravo. It's necessarily not a smart thought to participate as a primary concern game with a Master Manipulator. The best activity is to call them on their behavior and be immediate and direct. Control is an unpretentious type of harassing, and to face a harasser, you should be quiet and pleasant, yet exceptionally firm.

CHAPTER SIX

Manipulation in Relationships

Photoshop or advanced picture altering programming is used to manipulate pictures to appear to be unique from the first or to give the image a look which you want. Manipulation is the same, and it's tied in with controlling a person or a situation to get what you need. Why? A lot of things could cause this behavior.

Do you wind up doing things that you would prefer honestly not to? When someone near you or in power recommends that you accomplish something without wanting to, how would you feel?

Many people use manipulation as a way of controlling people, occasions, and their own lives. It's a kind of self-preservation component. Typically, these people who attempt manipulative tricks had no control as babies, regularly manhandled or deserted, and so on. Or on the other hand, in adulthood, they accept manipulation is a method for getting what they need. Utilizing the trick gives them power, and power feels euphoric.

Checkmate is a game position in chess where a player's king is undermined with catch, and there is no way to counter the risk. Or on the other hand, basically, the king is under direct assault and can't abstain from being captured. Comparative is the round of manipulation, to make a situation wherein the other person is caught and defrauded.

To manipulate someone is to play with someone's brain. You attempt to persuade the other person that what you are recommending is the best alternative for him. However, you realize it will work to support you.

For instance when Zora disclosed to her mother she would go to her in-laws place if she is a weight for them, she comprehended what will be the answer from her folks and she got what she needed and just remained for a considerable length of time together by making her parents feel remorseful of asking her to return to her home.

The manipulator sees himself at the focal point of the universe, and different things spin around him. He is content with the feeling of proprietorship and ownership of everything, feels little compassion for other people, and does little for others except if there is a personal preferred position.

The trick is to remember it and guarantee that you are neither a manipulator nor being manipulated, as this speaks to a dysfunctional relationship. Here are a couple of ways to know if someone is attempting to manipulate you:

1. **Tears**: When someone wells up with tears in his eyes, it doesn't mean their absolute tears.

2. **Discipline**: Withdrawing affection and backing.

3. **Untruth**: Manipulators are talented liars. They make up stories that sound coherent to make people feel frustrated about them so they can get something.

4. **Redirection**: Manipulator not offering a straight response to a straight inquiry and guiding the discussion to another point.

5. **Adulating** You: To get their way, manipulators will frequently make you feel better so they would then be able to request that you accomplish something that they need.

6. **Anger**: Manipulator uses anger to for enthusiastic power to get the unfortunate casualty into accommodation.

7. **Guilt trip**: This manipulative behavior tries to make you feel regretful.

To identify manipulative behaviors, consider what they do and whether their words are utilized to get you to accomplish something that you honestly would prefer not to do. Pose yourself a couple of inquiries about the motivation behind their activities.

When you identify the manipulator, make an intelligent decision of either cutting off from him or overlook him. Remain your ground and don't endeavor to contort and figure out how to state 'No.'

CONTROL THROUGH CONFUSION AND COMPULSION

In any sensibly sound relationship between couples, there is about in every case some cognizant or oblivious manipulation and intimidation. Be that as it may, relationships, for the most part, develop towards some parity if they are to stay steady and reliable.

In a profoundly manipulative relationship, the level of influence is solidly in the manipulator's camp. The manipulator opposes all endeavors to adjust the relationship-since they need unlimited authority, now and again by making their victim think they have some control.

The most noticeably awful relationships happen when an exceedingly manipulative individual enters a relationship with somebody exceptionally prone to manipulation.

The consciousness of how manipulation works, and of what makes a victim prone to manipulation, will help people break free from the move of duplicity they get captured in.

The trap is opened.

The starting sentimental, manipulative relationship is vague from some other. The manipulator gives visit positive strokes, particularly when their victim demonstrations in the way they wish to develop.

It is difficult to perceive any difference at this phase to a typical sentimental relationship. The two partners usually are mindful to one another, giving regular affirmation and positive strokes. Also, they rush to get things done for the other.

If not, things are headed toward a terrible start, as of now.

Sooner or later, the victim has been adapted to positive reinforcement (recollect, people who are progressively powerless to manipulation frequently have low confidence and are regularly people pleasers). Hello, and we as a whole like positive reinforcement and assertion that we are extraordinary to somebody.

Presently, the manipulator ordinarily starts to lessen the positive strokes.

Around this time, the manipulator will likewise start tossing in specific actions to befuddle their partner. They will start to grin less and may look exhausted with the victim. A typical strategy is to stroll around the house with a glare, making their 'partner' feel restless about what they may have done. Asking the manipulator will typically get the victim a 'nothing is the matter...Why?'

The general purpose is to muddle the victim and make them restless.

The victim is currently entering the unsure stage; regularly, things appear to go well; however, from time to time, they seem to have started on a crazy ride of vulnerability. The stress levels have begun to construct.

The goad is put in the trap.

Around this stage, the manipulator regularly lures the trap. An immediate or hidden idea of a significant reward is made. At work, it could be the potential for advancement or a continuous activity. It may be the idea of sex in individual relationships, or maybe the likelihood of marriage.

Numerous men will be comfortable with the-come here, leave, come here, leave, come here, leave ladies that keep them moving. Additionally, innumerable ladies have moved to the potential draw of a marriage for a considerable length of time. The switch of these jobs moreover happen.

What's more, everybody is powerless to the carrot of more significant compensation and advancements at work.

The guarantee of the big reward ordinarily brings recharged exertion and excitement, what's more, restored confidence in the relationship or profession in the brain of the victim.

The manipulator can utilize the big carrot and the big stick now. An implied threat of withdrawal of the 'prize' is periodically used to expedite expanded weight the victim, to keep them dubious and consistent.

Presently, the victim's stress levels have expanded further. They are questions about their relationship and future. The harder they work in their activity or relationship, the less and fewer rewards they appear to get.

Creating compulsive behavior

At this point, the manipulator is well while in transit to have the victim well and tangled in their strings. The monotonous routine of manipulation and the stress and vulnerability in the victim keep them from seeing and stepping back the big picture of what is occurring them.

Outside onlookers will frequently (however not generally) see checked differences in the character of the victim when they are within sight of the manipulator, to when they are in an increasingly typical relationship.

In any case, this is certainly not a clear pointer. Generally, the manipulator will modify their behavior when others are near, with the goal that the relationship seems increasingly adjusted. The victim may not understand why they are frequently more joyful when they are in other organization.

Manipulators, as a rule, have a fine sense for their victim's passionate state. If it starts to ascend for a long time, they will hose it down — continually yo-yoing their victim's feelings.

At this point, the victim might be adapted by intermittent and random threats and rewards. These are given with no apparent link to the victim's behavior. This kind of treatment can make a condition of compulsive behavior in the victim.

Researchers have found that people (and creatures) can create compulsive behaviors when they get rare and random rewards or threats.

While there is a clear link between an action and a reward, an individual more often than not stops that action rapidly, when the bonus stops. However, when constant and predictable rewards for a response is changed gradually to inconsistent and random rewards, people regularly prop the work up long after they got their last award.

Another variety for creating compulsive behavior in victims is to utilize intermittent and regularly random negative strokes. Shouting, annoying, and misuse is usual. When the victim is delicate and is dubious what prompts this behavior from their 'partner,' they tread lightly.

Gradually, through intermittent and random utilization of little positive and negative strokes, and progressively rare utilization of the big stick and carrot, the manipulator annihilates increasingly more of their partner's feeling of self. What's more, the victim turns out to be increasingly stressed. Without acknowledging, they are frequently gotten in compulsive behaviors that they would think odd if they saw it being finished by others.

Synopsis

We are for the most part prone to manipulation somewhat, however some substantially more so than others.

If you are prone to manipulation, the initial step to breaking free is to perceive the indications of manipulation in others.

The subsequent step is to start to comprehend what makes you powerless to manipulation.

The third step is to start to comprehend what is being done to you. For example, utilizing the intermittent random carrot and stick treatment to befuddle, bewilder, and stress you.

The fourth step will be to learn obstruction methodologies.

Are You a Victim of an Emotional Manipulator?

It is secure to say that you are afraid of conflict with your significant other or friend? Do you settle on awful decisions to oblige him? Do you lie to avoid issues? Do you reprimand yourself for his dissatisfaction? Do you race to spoil him when he winds up irritated? Do you give and sacrifice, give, give-and still feel dismal and desolate?

Maybe you are under the thumb of a specialist at emotional manipulation.

An emotional manipulator (EM) unobtrusively and sometimes subconsciously controls and manipulates the vulnerabilities of others-paying little heed to their needs-for his very own gain. He needs to oversee you. He utilizes devious techniques to change your perceptions, regularly without you knowing it. Extremely skilled emotional manipulators get you to give up your emotional confidence. When you put your very own prosperity into an EM's hands, he methodically chips away until there's almost no left of the original you.

How would this be able to happen to you, and what kind of individual turns into an emotional manipulator?

Many EM's are narcissistic and feel a feeling of entitlement given their upbringing or genetics or a combination. As children, their folks may have exposed them to similar emotional maltreatment. Or then again, oddly, these children may have been over-indulged or ignored. Boundaries of either may push a child into narcissism in later life.

A narcissist's entitlement makes them feel they ought to have what they need without earning it. There is no need for them to assume liability for themselves or their behavior. They don't need to be straightforward or even treat others fairly. It's about them and what the world has done to them.

So how is it that a beautiful individual like you can fall under the spell of an emotional manipulator?

It could be you are mutually dependent and attracted to an emotional manipulator. Neither of you likes to be separated from everyone else. If you are mutually dependent, you need to be needed. You need to help individuals. Deal with somebody. What's more, the emotional manipulator needs somebody to deal with him.

It's so natural to fall for the EM who establishes intimacy with you right away. He imparts profound emotions to you, and you perceive him as delightfully sensitive, open, and maybe a bit powerless. You need to support him. What's more, you get involved.

From that point onward, you are snared, and you don't notice you are emotionally manipulated. One week from now, I'll speak progressively about how to identify the behavior of an EM and how to extricate yourself from his grip on you.

The Four Styles of Emotional Manipulation

Everybody later or sooner in their life will have felt the icy grip of an emotional manipulator reaching inside to a piece of them which they feel unfit to safeguard regardless of how hard they attempt.

A manipulator aims to do only that, manipulate! The aim of their game is to gain control of the individual who is their picked victim; the explanation behind this is if they gain control of the other, at that point that individual can be made in numerous ways flexible to the manipulators desires, in this way reducing any danger to the manipulator Usually however, it is merely the manipulator paranoia and low regard which goes crazy in their mind giving them the impression that anybody and everybody is, or could be a risk.

To beat this and to guard themselves in their mind; they will attempt to trick the picked victim into feeling powerless, so whether the victim was to attack, they would more often than be not able.

There are four main types of the manipulator to watch out for, and these are

The Rejecter

This manipulator is a particularly dreadful one and is cutting straight profoundly of the most profound dread of 95% of humankind, which is that of being distant from everyone else. This dread is wrecking to the point that individuals will do pretty much anything to avoid it, including trying to win the manipulators affection.

The Insulter

This type of manipulator is "the jovial one" continually cracking the odd joke to a great extent, remarks about weight gain/misfortune, hairlessness and whatever other zone that the victim feels hesitant about, however then when the victim says how they feel, the manipulator returns with "I'm just kidding" or "don't get so stirred up" (a hit and run attack).

The Intimidator

This style is progressively visible. However, they will likewise attempt to keep it inconspicuous. This style of manipulation works by outstanding or straightforward changes in the body language, heavier breathing, displaying outrage, turning endlessly, raised voice or an appearance of they are prepared to attack. A change made frequently enough using a similar example yet without knowing why might regularly leave a victim befuddled and tense fearing the beginning of physical violence.

The nice person

This manipulator is by a wide margin one of the most devious. Posing as a friend and giving the impression that they are on the victims side, gradually gain their trust and willingness to open up the heart and after that unobtrusively drop in the degrading remarks and how despite the fact that the victim is an incredible friend a portion of their views and interests simply are not right and afterward the manipulator will seal the attack with, I'm just telling you since I care, giving the victim the appearance somebody to feel upheld by and go to when out of luck, however in all quintessence making them subordinate.

The manipulator is sometimes the very in the face types (physical violence) however the most unsafe; are the emotional types who get inside their victim's mind, hijacking their emotions leaving them confounded and helpless, giving the manipulator all the power. If you feel awkward around somebody yet don't have the foggiest idea why, the odds are you are in their grip and in numerous cases the two parties are ignorant, yet it is your responsibility to stop the game.

Persuasion and Manipulation

For more than ten years, I've trained sales and client administration at a neighborhood professional school. Unavoidably, my class and have long dialogs on the morals of sales, the significant of sales; how the sales procedure is used in each relationship and circumstance, why sales have such terrible notoriety, why great sales professionals aren't just paid liars. As a rule, our dialogs come back to one fundamental idea. Persuasion without respectability is only an extravagant name for manipulation. On the off chance that you're not clear on the difference:

Manipulation incorporates making people feel in charge of your success and happiness, making people accomplish something that they clearly would prefer not to do, making people accept an untruth so they will do things your way, and making people feel deficient except if they see the world how you do.

Controllers use the feelings of people against them, crushing trust simultaneously. People use manipulation because they don't have anything better to sell. What controllers offer the world isn't advantageous, or they wouldn't require manipulation to provide it with. Manipulation makes the life unnavigable and sinks everybody it hits.

Persuasion, conversely, endeavors to show people that they're in charge of their success and happiness. Belief attempts to help people discover the mental courage to do what they have to do, to see the outcomes of their activities, and to choose their actions carefully. People use persuasion because it encourages them to exhibit what they bring to the table in wording most straightforward for others to digest.

Persuasion mainly causes you to get a reasonable got notification from a something else, excessively passionate person. In persuasion, regardless of whether people choose to digest what you bring to the table, them remains their decision. You should never deny people their entitlement to decide for themselves. Your success in affecting another will eventually rely on the amount they esteem your offering. The more you offer them, the more they will respect you. Remember that idea as you endeavor persuasion for the duration of your life.

Simply after my understudies comprehend the difference between manipulation and persuasion are they ready to ace the instruments of impact...

THE ART OF STRATEGIC PERSUASION

- Are you meeting a delegate from one of your providers and need to arrange new evaluating with them?

-Have you acquired a useless group taking a shot at a prominent venture? How would you bring them around to working all the more cohesively and profitably?

Do your co-workers control information and assets that you have to satisfy your ventures and are not forthcoming or supportive?

- Do you have another idea to put before your supervisor, who is known to state 'no' before even completely listening to anybody?

- Do you need to develop 'champions' inside the association to help elevate your ideas to others?

- Do you need to be seen as increasingly alluring?

If you reacted 'yes' to any of these inquiries, you are a prime possibility for honing your forces of persuasion.

It's never again enough to 'tell' others what to do. Viable initiative these days relies upon your ability to influence key idea pioneers, senior administration, and cross-utilitarian groups. A persuasive argument is necessary, however just if you convey it with the confidence that comes from having gotten your work done.

The procedure of persuasion starts with how you consider the people you have to influence. Your accomplishment in influencing others relies on your ability to communicate and collaborate successfully and deliberately with them. Seeing how to shift frames of mind and practices brings about positive outcomes for everybody.

Before presenting a portion of the components that structure the reason for a persuasive argument or introduction, let me make a little however significant moral refinement, in particular, the difference among persuasion and control.

Being forthright, straightforward, and honest will furnish you with the establishment for reliable, trusting, and durable connections. Utilizing coercive or manipulative strategies may serve transient objectives. However, people won't react to mercifully as time goes on. Control is the improper use of the standards of persuasion. That is all — end of the story.

Then again, persuasion acquaints compelling recognition with others. This depends on the reason that people can do or consent to what they have first envisioned. The persuader's errand is to get others to envision doing what it is you need them to do. No coercion, no power, merely substantial information displayed such that bodes well. Here is a portion of the qualities and strategies that make a viable format for convincing others:

Intrigue BASED (otherwise known as What's In It For Me?)

-Position your arguments as far as how might this benefit your customers.

- Imagine things from the other's point of view.

- Understand what persuades and interests them.

SOCIAL PROOF

- People's ability to be influenced relies upon the social verifications that we call tributes.

- Use instances of how other clients have profited by your administrations/items.

Governmental issues

- This methodology depends on discovering others to support your idea.

- Highly competitive people and independent people will, in general, drive their ideas through all alone and don't use this type of persuasion to such an extent.

- Cooperative and gathering focused people look for support from others to advocate their ideas, regularly before the meeting even starts.

THE POWER OF LESS

- Offer just three solutions. Your client, manager, or customer will be increasingly well-suited to choose, and the center quite often wins. So, outline your solutions that way.

- More choices confuse your clients that outcome in their delaying for pushing ahead.

Discernment

- Using contemplated discussion, proof, and rationale to support your proposition will help guide move people towards a resolution.

- The more contemplated and consistent your solution sounds, the more prominent the possibility they will say yes.

Motivation and Emotion

- Using story-telling, pictures, and pictures will help move your customers inwardly.

- Studies by Wharton, in conjunction with IBM, explored that you are 38% bound to influence when you use visuals.

- Make your accounts contact the core of clients.

Connections

- Sharing something in common separates dividers.

- The more comparative you are to your colleagues and customers, the more persuasive the message becomes.

THE LIKABILITY FACTOR

- Positive connections incline your customers to be increasingly open to and supportive of your ideas.

- The more you are enjoyed, the more likely others will support your ideas.

- You're bound to be excused for mix-ups when you have championed.

THE LAW OF RECIPROCITY

- Your customers will be influenced to accomplish something for you when they first observe you performing something uncommon for them.

THE PROXIMITY EFFECT

- After a favor is done, your customers will put a higher incentive on the support than you. In any case, the pattern inverts. The estimation of the favor increments in your eyes as the practitioner and not in the eyes of the taker. So don't hold up everlastingly to bring in your markers.

Shortage

- Your customers will demonstrate a more prominent want and enthusiasm for something when they become familiar with its availability is restricted. Search for people to gobble up Pontiac autos since the line will be discontinued.

- Placing limits on amount accessible and confined timetables induce people to act all the more rapidly.

FOOT IN THE DOOR

- Evidence proposes that in the wake of consenting to a solicitation, your customers are bound to assist once more.

- They consider themselves to be committed to you and will be open to a bigger solicitation.

CHAPTER SEVEN

How to Influence People Successfully

To achieve extraordinary execution and efficiency from your staff, you need to work on your power of influence. Leaders were great at affecting whole things quicker and with insignificant exertion. When you become a constructive influence on your people, you will see a difference in outlook among them as they will feel profoundly energetic, excited in their work and take responsibility for obligations. To achieve this state isn't a simple undertaking and would expect you to build up the accompanying three skillsets.

Know your goal before you start your voyage

Influence is immaterial as it depends mainly on transit people think. How an individual thinks will drive his/her conduct, which thus influences his/her emotions. As a leader, you need to be influential in your reasoning with the end goal that you can change the mentality of the people that you lead. One case of this is the late South African

President Nelson Mandela. When he was discharged from jail following 27 years on scrounged up charges, his essential expectation was to unify the country who have been minimized along racial lines. To do this, Mandela connected with the South Africans to welcome each other through games and different exercises to evacuate any distrust and falsehood among his people of various racial sources.

To have this sort of influence would expect you to have a clear goal of where you need to go and why you need to go there. When you are clear of this, you need to work on your sympathy to comprehend what your people need and how you can synchronize this with your very own goal. You can achieve this by building a relationship of trust with the people you lead to such an extent that they consider you to be consistent with them through various challenges. When your people trust you, they will tail you where you need to go.

Focus on your ears, not your mouth

Greek philosopher, Zeno of Citium, stated: "We have two ears and one mouth, so we ought to listen more than we state." The power to influence is based on your ability to listen equitably and honestly. When you look to what your people need to state, you are accidentally building a meaningful long haul relationship. Further when you begin listening you will likewise purchase in for your thoughts as your people are set up to listen to you this way and in this procedure you could combine their places of perspectives with yours and work towards a success win circumstance that advantages everybody. This, at that point, will decrease clashes that stifle profitability and proficiency. Business visionary and Multi-billionaire Richard Branson is an extraordinary backer of listening and said compactly: "Listen, take the best. Leave the rest."

Figure out how to persuade like Aristotle

The last skill set to be a decent influencer is to ace the craft of persuasion. The difference between these two interlinked words is that influence is increasingly about building a relationship, trust, and accomplishing long haul objectives while belief is more towards being value-based, focused, and to achieve momentary goals. As a leader, sometimes, you do need to stand firm in that the condition that you are confronting would expect you to think of a snappy activity plan that does not enable you to consult with your people and influence them. This is the place you need to work on the power of persuasion. In any case, if you have set up the past two skillsets above, influencing people to achieve your momentary target would not be an issue.

Aristotle, in his work 'Talk,' identified three significant variables that you need to focus when you need to persuade anybody. He calls this: ethos (credibility), pathos (enthusiastic), and logos (intelligent). In a general sense, this means the main thing you need to persuade is by utilizing your character of being aware, genuine, and dependable (ethos). Next is to persuade by engaging their feelings by giving them a creative effect of how they will profit if they do what you are asking them (pathos). Anyway an expression of alert here is this is can be exposed to manhandle and all things considered you must be cautious by remembering the last factors which are to persuade by engaging their astuteness by giving them the essential statistical data points that enable them to settle on a choice about whether they would need to oblige you or not (logos). For whatever length of time that this is finished with credibility (ethos), you will achieve your final product effectively.

At last, as a leader, you are in control and how your people see you is mainly based on how you can influence them emphatically and energetically. This is when you leave an enduring inheritance.

Emotion Of Others

With regards to communication, what you hear is just a small amount of what's being said — much the same as an ice shelf, most of what's being imparted lies underneath the surface. Perusing individuals' emotions resemble a compelling artwork, and acing this skill can improve your compassion and comprehension of those with whom you associate. Systems administration, negotiating, child-rearing, contending, experiencing passionate feelings for – every one of these aspects of life is represented by enthusiastic articulations, and can be muddled when you experience difficulty reading these articulations.

Figure out how to peruse others' feelings by searching for prompts in both their nonverbal and verbal language.

1. Comprehend that words don't tell everything. With regards to reading others' emotions, if you wager all your money on words and don't think about different elements of communication, you will regularly lose the message.

Research considers you have bantered for quite a long time over the proportion of significance of verbal versus nonverbal communication. Some individuals have ventured to such an extreme as to state that words are just 7% of communication. This is false; coincidentally, however, the exact figures don't matter.

What does make a difference in your capacity to perceive that you shouldn't concentrate possibly on words when endeavoring to recognize another person's passionate temperature. Focusing on vocal assortment and body language are similarly as significant.

2. Tune in for tone of voice. If you have ever had somebody state to you "It's not what you stated, it's the way you said it," at that point, the individual was alluding to your tone of voice. Your sound is impacted by your cultural and semantic foundation, the unique circumstance, your relationship with another, and, shockingly, your state of mind. Although words themselves tell a great deal, the way, you state the words can convey a radically unique message to the recipient.

For instance, a husband touches base at home, and his better half says, "I see you worked late again today. You should have a requesting timetable this week?" How the spouse sees this message can vary by the spouse's tone. If she says it in a concerned, delicate tone, he may accept she is stressed over him and choose to open up and inform her regarding his day. If she said it in a judgmental, wry tone, in which the words are overstated, what's more, the tone is higher toward the last; he may accept that she's furious, so he closes down. Or then again more terrible, he may state something similarly sarcastic in response.

Tone can be portrayed as the attitude behind your words. While the sound is displayed verbally, it can likewise be handled as a part of body language.

In general, softer tones are related with a kind disposition and good manners, while a harsher tone may be related to resentment or negativity.

3. Focus on the individual's pitch. Pitch identifies with the relative highness or lowness of the individual's voice. A change in angle can influence the passionate tone of an individual's message.

For instance, when an individual's pitch is level and constant with no pronunciation, it frequently implies a lack of engagement or weariness with a theme - and furthermore exhausts the audience members.

4. Attribute significance to pauses that happen amid speech. Written communication has the joy of accentuation to enable the peruser to track and understand the planned importance. Spoken dialogue, in comparison, relies on pauses as a form of verbal accentuation. At the point when a speaker uses stops, he can make emphasis on certain words or expresses or impart humor and emotion.

An apprehensive individual may talk rapidly and run sentences together without delay.

An entertainer may share the initial segment of a joke, and permit a long delay, before catching up with the tagline. This gives the group of spectators' times to process the fun and after that, giggle suitably.

How To Understand Body Language

People get on what we genuinely think about whether we know it or not. One way we convey our thoughts is in our body language. The body can't lie. Lie locator tests depend on this fact. Although we, utilizing our conscious personality, can rest and we frequently do, our collection always enrolls the fact that we are lying.

The insider facts of body language imply that we may attempt to put on a bogus front to conceal our genuine feelings; however, our body is unequipped for lying. Conduct pros propose that solitary 7% of correspondence is the words we express. The rest is comprised of 38% tonality and 55% body language. When our words aren't compatible with our thoughts, it goes over in our tonality and our body language.

Some of the time people who are lying won't meet our look, kids do this a great deal, yet here and there great liars purposely hold the look of the person they are talking to as a way of concealing the fact they are as a rule not precisely honest.

A specialist in body language will see different things, for example, squint rate going up or anxious quirks. Mostly get the feeling that the person isn't harmonious; there's something not right. It's only a general feeling, yet its one trust.

People's motions give away their actual intentions. Many of us don't have the foggiest idea of how to peruse body language and don't understand how our very own physical developments address others.

Be that as it may, while we will most likely be unable to translate the intentions of others intentionally, unknowingly we get everything. This frequently drives us to feel uneasy with specific people.

Thoughts even convey themselves into letters, messages, and messages. Whatever your intention when you compose any of the above, it goes over to the person who gets the message.

Thoughts are conveyed in any medium, and a decent way of communicating as the need should arise is to initially think what result you might want from the letter, content, or email. Whatever you are feeling will run over regardless. Consider it first; then the correct words will come to you.

One day, someone was talking to a kindred specialist, and she disclosed to me that she had sent an email to a partner whom she was not precisely content with. Her prevailing thought as she composed the email seemed to be, "he would prefer not to insult her."

Learn to expect the unexpected. The person who got the email was insulted, and she said so in her answer. My companion couldn't comprehend why this had occurred yet when he disclosed to her how her mind functions and called attention to her overwhelming thoughts as she composed it, she understood what she'd done.

He proposed that next time she needed to compose an email of that sort, or any type so far as that is concerned, she initially records what she needed to accomplish as a result of the email. He asked her what she would have liked to occur.

She revealed to me that she needed to tell the other person that she wasn't content with what had occurred; however, she likewise required to do it such that smoothed over the agitated waters.

What proposed was that she would record, "he needs to develop an affinity with this person and to convey my regard for their perspective. He needs to be heard and to communicate as the need should arise in a way that makes a success, win circumstance. As a result of this email, He needs to stay firm companions and acquire a more noteworthy comprehension." She currently utilizes this technique with extraordinary achievement.

When comprehended the insider facts of body language can be utilized by you to get the results you need by being consistent and talking just about what you need to accomplish. Rolling out Positive Improvements can assist you with making the progressions that will made the best of your life.

LIST OF MANIPULATION TECHNIQUES

The Manipulation Process:

Different tactics are utilized in the manipulation process. Some are unmistakable, and others are too inconspicuous to even think about exploring or too complex to even think about analyzing.

i. Instillation of Guilt:

They see that the victim even admits of his issues and apologizes and feels humiliated superfluously. Step by step, they make the victim accepts they are bad enough, they couldn't care less enough, or they are narrow-minded, unforgiving, exploitative, and even parasitic. Much of the time, the manipulator has the vast majority of these highlights. The victim cannot look judiciously to see this isn't accurate because he/she has been customized into self-question, self-fault, and glorification of others together with devaluation of self.

ii. Disgracing:

A manipulator utilizes tactics to make the victim feels dishonorable, despicable and lacking so that there will never be a way out. If the victim attempts to challenge a manipulator, the last makes the victim feels embarrassed by terrorizing, dread, guilt and self-question, with an allegation of lack of capacity to do anything, lack of stamina, of power or mental fortitude. Mockery, jokes, criticism, and negative remarks, or even just dangers might be utilized. Once in a while, the manipulator incites the victim into a demonstration of aggression out of dissatisfaction and agony. This generally neglects to free the victim. Be that as it may, the manipulator would utilize such occurrence to make the victim feels further disgrace, disappointment, and guilt.

ii. **Gaining Sympathy:**

The manipulator may play the job of the victim to gain sympathy and participation if other tactics come up short. Summoning empathy, pity, and compassion from somebody reliable isn't tricky all things considered persons cannot stand seeing somebody who is enduring or in torment. The manipulator continues mourning how unfortunate they are, the way unreasonable things are, and how they are victims of such inhuman life.

iv. **Terrorizing:**

Dangers might be every day or incognito. A scary look, overlooking the other person, articulation of resentment or objection are a portion of the creepy demonstrations. Once in a while, it is pretending rage and a blast of feeling which is utilized to scare the person into accommodation. Dangers may run from outrageous conduct to destroy the economic wellbeing of the victim up to physical assaults and now and again threats to slaughter.

v. Enticement:

Sexual manipulation is utilized to give a misguided feeling of closeness and guarantee the obligation of the relationship. Emotional enchantment by bootlicking, acclaim and beguiling mentality can be immediately used to make the victims bring down their guards and gain their trust. This is typically fleeting and erratic, and through such irregular uplifting feedback, the victim is guided into the round of manipulation.

vi. Lying:

Lying is at the center of manipulation either by retention a significant measure of reality, discarding some significant certainties, or manufacturing false stories. The manipulator may overstate or limit actualities, cheat and betray the victim and assemble an unbelievable picture of himself, his victim, and their relationship. Blatant lying through denying "what you are discussing?" or professing to be absent-minded or confounded is once in a while utilized. Faking ailment or pain, fainting or false fits might be used to gain sympathy and debilitate the safeguards of the victim.

vii. Legitimization:

The manipulator may utilize different moves to clarify the purposes behind his conduct, which use the weakness of the victim. If the victim is guileless or incapable of passing judgment on a contention fundamentally, the manipulator may utilize vast numbers of the false notions of rationale to defeat his victim's counter-contentions. If the victim is ridden with guilt, disgrace or unforgiving inner voice, the manipulator utilizes all contentions which request to such vulnerabilities.

viii. **Denial:**

The manipulator may obtusely deny any wrongdoing or decline to let it out or dodge talking about the subject inside and out. He/she may take part in a meandering, superfluous befuddling talk which may occupy the consideration regarding a shocking question. Denial is different from lying if the person is uninformed halfway or entirely of reality.

ix. **Anticipating the fault:**

The manipulator may extend the responsibility on the victim, blaming him for vast numbers of his indecencies or here and there denounce others who have wronged him for the duration of his life and who made him what he is. The victim may feel either guilt, or he is put on edge to account for himself, or he may feel sympathy and distress for the manipulator.

x. **Aggression:**

The manipulator may fall back on genuine aggression and savagery to cause the victim to submit to his will, specifically if the victim is flimsier or disabled. This may leave an abrupt in a pretended upheaval of displeasure or extraordinary fierceness. Any reaction of a comparable sort from the victim is looked with progressively severe aggression which might be later accused on the victim himself, or a created sickness might be charged with just ascribed to the emotional issues the manipulator professes to confront.

CHAPTER EIGHT

Manipulation Techniques

We had taken in the craft of manipulation as far back as when we were newborn children. When an infant cry when her mother puts her to bed is one way of manipulation to get their way.
Manipulation is in the very center of each human. With the tremendous information, we have amassed until nowadays and with the regularly developing innovation that makes data simple to get to, learning the capacity to convince others is inside handle.

Controlling Techniques these days prove to be useful with the ascent of the web. Numerous people can investigate and contemplate the suppositions and encounters of the people far and wide. Getting the hang of controlling techniques do build your general self. Information and relational abilities, which is a significant fixing in our interaction and human relationship, can carry accomplishment to a person. For people who are professing to know the skill, yet don't generally realize how to actualize it, will begin ineffectively. Like this, knowing the basics on what can make or break your procedure is a significant technique, to start with.

Numerous techniques are utilized when it comes to controlling. A couple of messy traps are used by people to control others. Although consequently, they would likewise fall into difficulty of getting similar karma they purposefully practice.

There are a couple of manipulation techniques that don't include shrewd or misleading motions. Manipulation techniques are utilized generally to exceed the method of others yet, at the same time, using the objectives and principles of reasonable challenge. In business, we need to out-think our rivals by giving the best enthusiasm to our customers and noting the needs of our clients. We can stay aware of our challenge by moving ourselves to accomplish more and by getting bolster that we need in connection to personal growth.

We need to know that manipulation includes mind interaction since we can convince a person when we read his or her mind.

In a food chain don't act just as predators we are likewise prey for others; therefore, we need to realize that "Not all facts are truly true." People will, in general, put stock in things regardless of whether they are made to accept that it is true. When a sales rep is selling their item, they will make you receive that it is helpful. We need to understand that they are just utilizing manipulation techniques to get us in their way.

We additionally need to understand that "Being perfect is an inconceivability." Everyone means to be perfect, and would effectively change such imperfections. Once in a while, we can redesign or make something better, yet these progressions are as yet not correctly done. A brightening cream doesn't always give you the perfect white skin that you need to accomplish if you don't generally have a white appearance. Manipulation techniques possibly work longer when they depend on the real world.

PERSUASION VS MANIPULATION - WHICH ONE ARE YOU APPLYING?

Numerous learner direct reaction sales copywriters get mistook for utilizing the specialty of persuasion versus manipulation when creating points of arrival, sales letters, and messages to sell their products and services.

Manipulation is the applying mischievous impact for one's very own preferred position, through methods, for example, lying and being misleading...getting what you need from others notwithstanding when the others are not willing at first to offer it to you.

Manipulation is enticing for some people. This form of correspondence can be compelling and very incredible, yet... deceptive, unpleasant and directly downright off-base. Organizations running such battles utilizing this technique will be fleeting, and their notoriety will tank amazingly quick.

Utilizing manipulation on your prospects won't win you any pats on the back. The opportunity will feel constrained into a sale, and I ensure they won't wind up turning into a dependable client at any point shortly.

A genuine case of manipulation could be one of those phone specialist tricks who focuses on the old. Persuading dread strategies and ultimatums to swindle them out of their only remaining dollar, or direct such a fantastic controlling discussion, that powers the beneficiary out of their secret information. The individual, at last, feels vanquished and terrified not to do as told. Persuasion is the demonstration of impacting the brain by reasons offered, a form of social impact. Belief is intended to win the other individual over, expelling obstructions so they can arrive at their own decision, not to crush them.

This procedure is persuading your client to change his or her convictions as well as to conduct through reasonable or sensible methods instead of power. Sadly, persuasion is both famously difficult to dismantle off and practically to challenge to oppose when progressed admirably.

By applying the persuasion procedure in your sales copy, you will pick up trust and believability with your prospects. You enable them to pursue their very own decision about your product or service by being straightforward and earnestly helping them with a need or issue. What's more, people are additionally ready to acknowledge your message without considering every one of the certainties if you have certain qualities that make them have a sense of security:

Genuineness: Everyone cherishes a legit approach. It shows off your ethics and conditions, hence gaining you believability with your prospects who will keep on working with you. When composing your copy, don't utilize false proclamations or lies to sell your product.

Like Ability: People are effectively convinced into getting things done by others whom they like. Include your character or story into your sales piece. Tell the prospect of your identity. This, at last, forms, trust.

People additionally love to do things they see others doing. Spot individual when tributes into the progression of your copy. This informs your prospect that the "regular person" is doing it so for what reason right?

You never need to control your prospect, compelling them into purchasing your product or service, yet it's alright to influence them into settling on their own choice by giving them legit reasons and featuring the advantages of why they should buy.

Ensure if you are attempting to induce your prospect in your sales copy to make a specific move, you are utilizing it to impact them the correct way and for all the right reasons; helping them accomplish an ideal outcome or take care of their concern.

Joni's immediate reaction copywriting capacity collaborated with her inventiveness, and bright side unmistakably separates her on the quick reaction copywriting phase of today. She is in charge of transforming numerous stale private venture sales ventures into genuinely determined, contemporary, unique style of copy bringing about profoundly expanded sales transformations.

Empathic Abilities

Sometimes perplexing to tell whether someone is an empath, (a psychic who has empathic capacities). The issue is, you don't generally know if someone has these psychic forces, or if they are touchy, getting people. How would you know if you're incredibly empathic?

Empaths are very touchy to the feelings of everyone around them. Frequently, an empath will probably sense what someone is encountering, regardless of whether they can't see or hear that person. Someone with this kind of ability, basically "knows." Many psychics with empathic capacities report encountering someone else's feelings just as they were their own. However, this isn't generally the situation.

A psychic with this kind of ability will most likely sense the feelings of others, mainly if those feelings are reliable. Underlying feelings that an empath will experience incorporate dread, bliss, sadness, energy, love, and foreboding. The more grounded the passion, the simpler it will be for the empath to sense, comprehend, and feel.

What sets empaths separated from other, "normal" people, is that they have a more profound, progressively delicate comprehension for what they are feeling. This intuition originates from inside and is far more prominent than what a great many people understand. For instance, a "normal" person may realize that someone they love is resentful about seemingly insignificant details they state or do. Be that as it may, an empath would sense this even without seeing or conversing with that person, and an empath could sense if that loved one was feeling sold out, envious, furious, or hurt. This psychic intuition would originate from inside, not from the visual or capable of being heard signs of the physical world.

Empaths can tell when something isn't right, regardless of whether that something hasn't occurred at this point. They are overwhelmed with a profound sense of foreboding that cautions them that everything isn't as it ought to be. A "normal" person, then again, would not have the option to tell when something sudden or hazardous would occur.

These things all solid extraordinary; however, not every person understands that it can likewise be challenging to be an empath. This is because empaths are not ready to "shut off" their capacities whenever they need. That is, they can't pick whether to feel something. Instead, they should feel whatever their psychic intuition senses, regardless of whether they would prefer not. This is an enormous weight for empaths, and it is additionally why empathic psychics can become ill from weariness.

WHAT KIND OF EMPATH ARE YOU?

It is safe to say that you are an empath? You know you are touchy, and your most grounded mystic sense is in feeling. For entertainment only, take the test to discover which kind you are.

Hover in your mind or record which applies.

1. You catch a sharp, unpleasant stomach ache. Intelligent personality says it was an awful lunch or this season's flu virus going around; however, then your canine goes into the room and vomits on the rug. She looks somewhat green around the edges. (physical or animal empath)

2. While shopping at the adjacent Walmart, you enter the solidified food section and need to blast out into tears. You feel overpowering, profound misery, and depression. (passionate empath or sensitivity to ineffectively structured boxed foods)

3. While unwinding in the lounge chair, you all of a sudden hear words originate from your canine, "I need to take a walk now." (animal empath or the consequence of smoking an excessive number of mushrooms)

4. Sitting in the terrace you feel a flood of happiness come over you and a feeling of harmony, and you incline to smell the flower hedge (nature empath or the mushrooms are as yet doing their stuff from the day preceding)

5. You feel down and angry when two minutes before you thought quiet. Your dearest companion at that point calls and says he is feeling down and

furious. (enthusiastic empath or you just shopped at a swarmed Walmart)

6. Two days before a noteworthy earthquake hits another nation you have bad dreams of tremors, tension or feelings of fate (mission empath or observing an excessive number of motion pictures before bed)

7. You realize that one fern plant needs more water and to be put in a sunnier window (nature empath or you've perused a ton of books on houseplants)

8. You get reliable messages or channelings that will help the world concerning confidence (mission empath or still feel the impacts of the mushrooms)

9. You enter an emergency clinic and feel dread, bitterness, nervousness. You stroll by one room and feel torment in your side (physical empath or dread of clinics)

If you orbited at least one for nature empath: NATURE EMPATH you're fixed on the Nature Spirits and Fairies. You would exceed expectations at mending with Nature.

If you orbited at least one for passionate empath: EMOTIONAL EMPATH you're fixed on the feelings of others. You need to take a shot at discovering high devices and surprisingly better limits to exploit this gift.

If you circumnavigated at least one for physical empath: PHYSICAL EMPATH you're fixed on the physical diseases of others. You will need to observe how to dispose of the feelings and not take it on. You'd make a superb therapeutic natural.

If you orbited at least one for animal empath: ANIMAL EMPATH you're fixed on animals and can help them enormously if you support this capacity.

If you surrounded at least one for mission empath: MISSION EMPATH you're fixed on the world, and your gifts will be utilized to help the planet on a more noteworthy scale.

If you orbited mushrooms: Whoa! Where did you get that stuff?

Empathic Psychic Abilities - Psychic Guide
What are Empathic Psychic Abilities?

An empathic psychic is otherwise called an "empath." Empaths can detect and encounter the feelings of others, like the way telepaths can detect the contemplations of others. Empathy and clairvoyance are firmly related to psychic abilities.

Typically, clairsentient psychics, (psychics with "clear feeling"), have empathic psychic abilities. Empathic abilities are rare, yet not unbelievable.

Characteristics of an Empath

Empaths display these characteristics:

- Extraordinary affectability to the feelings of others
- An intense consciousness of their environment
- Clear comprehension of body language
- Solid information about human feeling
- The ability to feel further than others
- The Empathic Spectrum

Not all psychics have a similar measure of empathic power. A few psychics have just necessary empathic abilities, while others have amazingly progressed empathic skills. Most empaths fall someplace in the center.

Psychics with the most basic empathic abilities can detect what another is feeling, and can now and again feel their feelings. These psychics can see some of what others are feeling.

Psychics with the most progressive empathic abilities can feel everything that other's are feeling. When occupied with empathic practice, these psychics regularly become so drawn in individuals' feelings, that they quickly free sight of their personality. Psychics, for example, these might most likely send passionate flag and undertaking their feelings onto others.

Empathic Healing

Many empaths utilize their abilities to recuperate others. Empaths, as a rule, place their hands on somebody, to comprehend what they are feeling. Along these lines, an empath can concentrate legitimately in on what the patient needs.

Powerful empathic psychics can share the feelings of others, to mitigate their agony. Misfortune and sadness are two normal feelings that a powerful empath can share and reduce. To turn around this strategy, a psychic can likewise share their very own feelings to spread joy and bliss.

A Gift or a Curse?

Since empaths invest so much energy agonizing over the feelings of others, they can neglect to stress over themselves. Empaths may encounter weakness because of self-disregard, passionate pressure, and physical weariness.

Then again, mending and spreading feelings of joy is a rare and superb gift!

Ideally, you've gotten the hang of something about empaths and empathic psychic abilities.

Tools For An Empath's Energy Protection

Standard characteristics of an Empath and why they need protection:

Empaths are attracted to healing themselves and others. They are typically attracted to healing since they feel that they have so much inner healing to do... until that is, they understand that the majority of the healing required is for others, that they are naturally 'feeling.'

They are as a rule in a condition of consistent weariness. This is an enormous issue. People, alongside their energies, are always attacking an Empath's energy. An Empath will more often than not take on something over the top and become depleted all-around rapidly, and it's not effectively restored by rest or rest. It goes a lot further than that and is very debilitating.

Empaths are great audience members. They care about the prosperity of others and wind up tuning in to the burdens of people they don't know. A great many people discover Empaths so natural to open up to. That is when they begin dumping a wide range of pessimism going in their life. Sometimes, people aren't even mindful they are doing this.

By and large, an Empath with deal with the necessities of others even before their own, because they care to such an extent. Since people get settled enough around them to open up, they will more often than not sacrificially listen carefully to enable an individual; regardless of whether it's to their disservice.

Alone time is a need for an Empaths. Many Empaths like to make tracks in the opposite direction from the majority of the feelings and energy that isn't theirs, so they require essential time alone. This is time for them to return to balance, and separate themselves from all pessimism that isn't theirs.

An Empath can likewise show up as ill-humored. Empaths sometimes appear to have significant emotional episodes, and this sometimes is added to the majority of the staggering musings and feelings shelling them every day. Not exclusively are they bombarded with these energies, yet now they have to deal with and make sense of all that stuff coming their way.

They are sincerely touchy to savagery, mercilessness, or any catastrophe. Most Empaths quit viewing the TV and perusing the papers sooner or later in their lives, as this as well, can be overpowering for an empath.

Out and out knowing is additionally a typical Empath attribute. Empaths sometimes know things that they are sure they were never instructed or told. This knowing is altogether different than instinct or a warning.

Being in open places is frequently overpowering or agonizing to an empath. Again such a large number of people's feelings are in public places that can be gotten when not by any means attempting to. This is a crazy ride most Empaths will maintain a strategic distance from no matter what.

An Empath can 'feel' genuineness and honesty. They can tell if someone is being straightforward or not, which is very agitating and sometimes confusing in your life. It's particularly agitating when they are managing friends and family.

Feeling the physical manifestations and agonies of another. Numerous Empaths will end up building up a disease that someone else has that has nothing to do with them. This is empathy at its best.

These are only a couple of the characteristics of an Empath. Once more, being an Empath can be either viewed as a revile or a gift contingent upon the apparatuses you use to secure yourself. There are numerous ways for Empaths to Protect themselves. Staying away from huge parties or open places, no matter what is one way. In any case, there are times when you can't keep away from these things. There are many useful ways to secure yourself as an empath. This is what I like to keep in what I call 'My Bag of Tricks': I use Crystals, Meditation, and The White Light of Protection.

CRYSTALS

Rose Quartz is an incredible crystal for an Empath because its healing properties advance unrestricted love and solace. This is particularly useful for an individual that might hold not exactly adoring energies of something, someone, or even themselves.

Dark Tourmaline or Hematite are additionally incredible crystals for an Empath to enable them to remain grounded. These stones will likewise retain any negative energies.

Malachite is another crystal that will help assimilate any negative feelings you might have; regardless of whether they are your own or not!

Labradorite is a crystal that will help shield your emanation from engrossing any issues that are being imparted to you.

Citrine is a yellow crystal to help light up your mind-set. other Citrine healing property is that it can likewise help ingest terrible energy from your condition.

Another go-to crystal for me is Amethyst. It is beautiful, it will reinforce your instinct. Elevated instinct is superb for everybody, except mainly for

Empaths to help them genuinely realize that the feelings they might have are theirs or not.

To wrap things up is Rainbow Fluorite. Rainbow Fluorite might be, as I would see it, the Mother of all crystals for an Empath as it helps all degrees of being! This is a multi-hued crystal that can enable you to remain grounded to the earth, help clear and balance all Chakras, just as to allow you to continue sensitive to higher measurements.

These are my go-to crystals to enable me to remain focused, grounded, ensured, and tuned in. Crystals can and will help recuperate your life!

Meditation

Meditation has been utilized for a great many years as a way to accomplish a degree of mindfulness that is past the constraints of the consistently thinking personality. Naturally, it's the act of uniting, the psyche, body, and soul!

Most don't understand that our bodies were intended to act naturally amending to keep up positive wellbeing by mostly keeping psyche, body, and soul in balance. Envision that it is so natural to be out of balance when the energy of others penetrates your body consistently. It's epic!

When you are out of balance, your life-force energy doesn't stream an incredible way it should. Being out of balance appears in life as a throbbing painfulness. What's more, when you are out of balance for a considerable length of time, your body starts to make ailment and infection.

Alone time and meditation is an excellent way for an empath to keep themselves balanced, sound, and entirety. This is simply the act of cherishing that most Empaths set at the back of the line if they even place it in the line of significance by any stretch of the imagination!

White Light of Protection

When I can't abstain from doing things that don't crest my 'wow meter, for example, going into huge groups, I for the most part attempt to ensure myself and my energy with 'White Light.' Numerous people do it any other way, and there's no set in stone way to do it because genuinely it's about the intensity of expectation.

Take a couple of minutes to yourself and sit in a calm place before you do anything. Close your eyes and take a couple of full breaths. On each in-breath, picture the white light of protection coming into your body through your crown and filling your whole existence. Keep taking in the white light and when your whole body is loaded up with light, envision that light currently sparkling splendidly and developing so enormous that it presently shines outside of you, encompassing your entire body. Sit breathing profoundly for a couple of minutes and feel light that encompasses you. Presently grin and have a touch of appreciation, since you've recently polished self-esteem by putting yourself first. Also, you've quite recently finished shielded yourself from all unwanted and negative energies around you!

These are only a couple of the ways that you can ensure yourself if you have an affectability to other energies. I trust this made a difference! Also, by and by, kindly offer any tips and deceives that you may have that I haven't referenced. Allows all assistance each other by sound and entirety!!

How to Manipulate People and Influence Decisions

Manipulation isn't moral, yet in this dog eat dog world, we need to realize how to manipulate people unpretentiously and impact their choices. Presently, I'm not saying you go out there and manage everybody you meet in the city. Use these techniques to your benefit. Here and there you can likewise use these techniques to accomplish positive results.

We will perceive how to impact utilizing manipulation unpretentiously. While it is impractical to introduce a well-ordered strategy as each circumstance is novel, there are a few rules you can pursue to actualize these thoughts. Specifically, there are three things you need to know about to get what you need effectively.

Above all else, you should attempt to infuse a compelling feeling when trying to manipulate somebody. It could be greed, dread, want, or any such sense. If you don't do this at that point, people will begin to think unmistakably, and your odds of progress will be remote.

Something else you need to know is the hot catches of the person you are attempting to manipulate. Via cautiously watching the person you will comprehend what is his/her hot trick. It could be a pet, side interest, or a solid inclination about a subject.

At long last, you need to know about social engineering techniques. Hackers use this a great deal to gain access to very verify frameworks. For example, if a person in a police uniform requests that you move far from a spot, will you proceed to look at if he is extremely a cop? We are adapted to react with a particular goal in mind to specific people. Like this, there are a few other social factors that you can use for your advantage.

In this way, since you realize the fundamental rules begin watching people and investigate circumstances and attempt to gain from them.

CHAPTER NINE
Learn How to Manipulate People

Despite whether you need to prevail at your specific employment, or in close to home connections, you should realize how to manipulate people. While the words may appear to have an illegal meaning, there is an unpretentious equalization that makes people progressively alluring. All things considered, if you try too hard, or don't have any significant bearing the rules accurately, chances are you will end up being the cliché "controller that everybody needs to dodge.

If you need to realize how to manipulate people without being oppressive, conversational hypnosis offers you the best organization. In addition to other things, you will learn essential traps to use during any conversation that will enable you to pick up an affinity and keep it. Much of the time, your group of spectators won't understand that you are utilizing a type of hypnosis to get what you need from them.

You might be pleased to discover that a portion of the people you regard the most naturally use a piece of these traps. Have you at any point gone into a circumstance vowing that you could never do or say something? Did you end up doing only that at an unimportant recommendation from another person? Chances are, at any rate at least one parts of conversational hypnosis was used.

Today, there is a wide range of approaches to figure out how to manipulate people. For instance, numerous frameworks depend on figuring out how to impart all the more viably, while others focus on utilizing guarantees and other motivating forces to get people to surrender to your will. Then again, conversational hypnosis will show you how to use your voice and body language to lull others into an increasingly pleasing state. Notwithstanding whether you need to manage a furious sentimental accomplice or a hostile administrator, conversational hypnosis can make it a lot simpler for you to guide the conversation into an all the more satisfying bearing. Chances are when you begin utilizing these strategies, and others will be stunned at how you generally figure out how to get what you need.

The Difference Between Manipulating and Inspiring Your Target Audience

For some of the first word, manipulation has negative undertones connected. However, the following word, inspiration, has an unmistakable positive ring. All things being equal, manipulation is usually related to accomplishing goals, while arriving at similar closures utilizing inspiration is something that is by all accounts inside the capacities of the few. You may use manipulation to attempt to get prospects to buy your item or administration. Manipulation works in the short term. Inspiration, be that as it may, turns out to be progressively crucial if you need to build up long haul relationships with your prospects or customers. So what is the difference between the two?

Manipulation

While manipulation sounds like an adverse action, a large portion of us does it consistently. In like manner, a large part of us is affected in our everyday activities and considerations by outside sources, even though be it intuitively. This, quality is an innate piece of our human necessary leadership process. Besides, manipulation can be confident. Numerous businesses use positive manipulation to impact customers. In his blockbuster "Impact: The Psychology of Persuasion" psychology and marketing expert, Robert Cialdini, clarifies how this is finished by applying at least one of the six critical standards of persuasion.

Here is a token of the six.

Correspondence - When you accomplish something for another person, they will probably need to give back where its due.

Commitment and consistency - Once an individual has focused on an action, they are more probable finish and respect the commitment.

Material evidence - People like to feel as though they have a place, so they will duplicate the conduct of others whose endorsement they look for.

Authority - People will, in general, pursue figures of authority.

Loving - People will confide in you more if they like you.

Shortage - When something is rare, the interest for it increments. Giving constrained offers or showing stock is low can assist potential customers with making a buying choice.

Manipulation can be exceptionally compelling. However, these techniques work on a short-term premise.

Inspiration

Because manipulation, or affecting (the favored term these days), works in the short term, you additionally need to consider long haul customer commitment. How might you rouse your customers to focus on your business for quite a long time to come? Approach yourself what your business relies on. What goals would you say you are attempting to accomplish with your business? You need to make cash, yet in a fruitful business making cash is a result, not a goal. In "Begin With Why: How Great Leaders Inspire Everyone to Take Action" creator and marketing consultant, Simon Sinek, advances his vision on progress through inspiration. As he would like to think, the inquiries that business owners ought to posture are the accompanying: "Why does your association exist? Why does it do the things it does? Why do customers truly buy from some organization?"

As a business owner, it is essential to know why your customers are yours or why somebody picked your business as a position of work. That is the difference between manipulation and inspiration. When you know the responses to that inquiry, you will have found what it is about your remarkable business, and that pulls in people to you. Activities that impart their convictions and goals are increasingly fruitful in manufacturing long haul relationships with customers.

At last, how might you make sure that your intended interest group peruses your message and follows up on it? Reveal to them why you do what you do before you disclose to them what you do and how you do it. Tell them why your business is different and make it individual. Motivate people with your story. Inspiration is a lot more dominant than manipulation. If you can get that and actualize it in the manner you advertise your business, there is no restriction to the statures you can reach.

How to Manage Manipulative People

I'm sure you can recollect an event when you've wound up accomplishing something with a friend that you honestly would not like to. If it happens all around sporadically, that is fine; it's merely a decent friend. Anyway, when it happens consistently, and you continue thinking about how it occurred, at that point, it's time to investigate the manipulative conduct and think about how to take control.

Manipulation is characterized as: 'The act of guiding somebody into ideal conduct to accomplish a shrouded personal objective.' Regularly we don't know it's transpiring as manipulative people can be extremely unobtrusive. Likewise, the nearness of feelings, for example, love, faithfulness, and trust, can mean we don't see the truth of other people's shrouded plans. It's effortless to be drawn in.

As you would expect, the limits of manipulative conduct can be found in TV programs which highlight narcissists, for example, Janine Butcher in Eastenders or Kirtsy Soames in Coronation Street. A manipulator at home or work can be progressively challenging to spot, regularly the main thing you perceive is a feeling of resentment, bothering, guilt, or perplexity.

Normal manipulative conduct:

· Buttering you up. In this situation, the person begins by disclosing to you how magnificent you are, or how well you accomplished something. This makes you feel high and less inclined to state no or to disillusion them.

· Guilt trip. This conduct is intended to make you feel guilty. You think that doing what the other person needs is something you 'should' do regardless of whether you don't have any desire to. Phrases utilized could be, "I'm continually getting things done for you... " or "I would do it for you..." or "if you were my friend you would... "

· Self-pity. Here the manipulator makes a long-haul propensity for being the person in question or the person who needs consideration. This guarantees you remain concentrated on them and stay active. Phrases utilized could be, "yet I'm so disliked/sick/troubled/futile...," or "my life is such a vast amount of harder than yours... "

· Isolating. To accomplish this, the manipulator will propose everybody concurs with their supposition and not yours. On the other hand, they will disclose to you that another person you know has said it is the correct thing to do, which pushes the duty away from them. Phrases utilized could be, "you're the one in particular who thinks that way... " or "your friend Katie revealed to me you ought to do... "

· Withdrawal. This is the utilization of shirking or the quiet treatment to get you to attempt and re-associate with them and to make you feel guilty.

· The Martyr. This person carries on as though they are being obliged to you, however really is mistaking being useful for the should be significant to you. By getting things done for you that you haven't requested, they increment the strain to return the support and for you to appreciate them. Phrases utilized could be, "I'll help you out... " or "I don't worry about, you pick... "

The critical thing to recall when figuring out how to adapt to manipulation is that no one has the privilege to manipulate or control your feelings without your consent. Hence it is essential to build up limits to ensure yourself inwardly.

People who want to manipulate are commonly poor and ward people who aren't happy with advancing their suppositions straightforwardly. Subsequently, they utilize these practices to get you to do what they need. You have sooner or later used one of these manipulative practices, the difference being that you would use them once in a while, as opposed to consistently, similar to a manipulator.

The most effective method to respond to manipulative conduct:

• **Don't be drawn into the guilt trip.** "I understand you figure I ought to do it, anyway right now it doesn't fit with my arrangements."

• **Clarify their comments**. "Who precisely do you mean when you state everybody thinks I should?"

• **State your feelings about their comments.** "I'm presently feeling befuddled/awkward about what you said... "

• **Assertively request what conduct you would prefer**. "When you state... it makes me feel guilty, I would prefer if you."

• **Don't be drawn into corresponding favors.** I welcome you were helping me, anyway I'd prefer not to do it later on as I will most likely be unable to return the support".

• **Positively react to self-pity**. "I can understand you're having a hard time with your better half/kids/sickness/work, yet isn't it incredible that you've... "

· **Stay quiet. Talk unmistakably**, in a calm tone and with no trace of judgment, whatever the other person's conduct.

If none of this is useful at that point, perhaps it's time you found different friends or associates who will treat you with real regard and lift your self-regard

Sometimes it's difficult to dissect our very own and others peoples conduct and ability to deal with a circumstance. Talking things through with an accomplished life mentor can genuinely help.

CONCLUSION

Passionate behavioral conduct standards show up, on its substance, to avoid some critical pieces of human brain science. Where are the mental, the exuberant, and explicitly the physical and resolutions? Enthusiastic standards of conduct seem to propose some inclination or feeling that fittings honestly into a show or some similarity thereof and depicts some foreseen line of horrid spreading out, sounding careless and detrimental.

No issues as yet, in our perception of passionate personal conduct standards. In any case, there is a spot for instinct, for essentialness, similarly concerning the human and compelling. Although these examples are not a distinguishing strength in social brain research, our view of human conduct, both interior and outside, drives us, sensibly soon, to watch the monotonous thought of people. Apparently, outward appearances, genuine sign, speed of advancement, game plan of conduct, standard of direct imparting regards and diversions, tendencies, inclinations, and level of care are adequate to make them heave our arms with frustration: how, how, and by strategies for what is the human-animal separated from any being whose mindfulness emanates from and is overpowered by the base chakras of dread, survival, having a spot, and verifying?

By and large, by a full edge, individuals live their lives in a condition of emergency, under principles of survival, dreading the most perceptibly horrendous, foreseeing failure, yearning for awful violence, dejection, shortage, imagining the assaults of time, the start of torment, calamity, and frustration - in this way, believing a fiasco of life a million times more awful than what will, almost certainly, ever transpire.

What are we to make of this? Do we genuinely live in a condition of franticness anything like the one we dread? Is our state of fear in any way proportional to the hazard introduced? Does our level of strain in any position address a better than average response to what may happen us?

Thanks for giving me confidence and took my book, if you want to read other fantastic books visit My Library ...

You won't regret it!

Made in the USA
Middletown, DE
13 March 2020

86302958R00102